Dawn from on High

Homilies for the Weekdays of
Advent, Christmas, and Epiphany

Holy Name 2015

To Arnold

With all best wishes and prayers

John D Alexander+

Cover: *Starfire in the East*, a 3-feet wide sculpture in burnished bronze, by David Orth. www.orthsculpture.com. Image used with permission.

Scripture quotations are from the New Revised Standard Version of the Bible, copyright © 1989 the National Council of the Churches of Christ in the USA. Used by permission. All rights reserved. Psalm passages are from the Psalter in *The Book of Common Prayer*.

All rights reserved.

ISBN: 978-0-88028-402-8

Printed in USA

© Forward Movement 2014

Dawn from on High

Homilies for the Weekdays of
Advent, Christmas, and Epiphany

John D. Alexander

Forward Movement
Cincinnati, Ohio

Introduction

A particular blessing for Episcopal congregations offering a daily Eucharist or Mass has been the availability in recent years of the Weekday Eucharistic Lectionary (not to be confused with the Daily Office Lectionary in *The Book of Common Prayer*, 1979). Before this resource became available, the choice of readings for daily eucharistic readings was often haphazard: one drew from those appointed for the various saints' days in *Lesser Feasts and Fasts*, the Propers for Various Occasions, (also known as Votive Masses) and, when all else failed, the readings from the previous Sunday.

In this book, I offer a series of homilies for the weekdays of Advent, Christmas, and Epiphany through the Baptism of Our Lord, based on the readings in the Weekday Eucharistic Lectionary. In 1994, the General Convention of The Episcopal Church directed that "the Psalms and Readings of the weekdays of Advent, Christmas, and the weekdays between the Feast of the Epiphany and the Baptism of Christ as they appear in *The Book of Alternative Services* of the Anglican Church of Canada be added to *Lesser Feasts and Fasts*" (Resolution 1994-A071). The Weekday Eucharistic Lectionary of the 1985 Canadian

Book of Alternative Services had in turn been adapted from that of the 1970 *Roman Missal*. *Holy Women, Holy Men: Celebrating the Saints*, a 2010 revision of *Lesser Feasts and Fasts*, also includes these additions to the lectionary.

My hope is that these homilies will prove helpful to preachers preparing weekday homilies during these seasons. Alternatively, those unable to celebrate or attend a daily eucharist may find them helpful as daily meditations for personal or group reflection.

I offer these homilies as a parish priest who regularly preaches at weekday eucharists. They are representative of the homilies I have given for a number of years at the daily Mass at Saint Stephen's Church in Providence, Rhode Island. I generally stay close to the scriptural texts. I am not a biblical scholar, but I aspire to be an "educated consumer" of biblical scholarship.

In seminary, most priests of my generation were taught to pay close attention to the historical context in which the biblical texts were written, on the assumption that understanding how the original readers heard the texts would facilitate the preacher's "hermeneutical leap" to how they might speak to us today. In the years since, I have learned to pay attention also to the Church's theological tradition of interpretation, beginning with the classic patristic commentaries. As I was writing the homilies for this book, I also made a conscious effort to interpret the texts in what might be called their "liturgical-seasonal" context: Why did the Church choose this particular text to be read at this particular time of year? How does this day's text (or juxtaposition of texts) illuminate the themes of the liturgical season? And how does the liturgical season illuminate the meaning of the text?

Writing homilies for Advent brings its own set of challenges. To preach effectively on the biblical hope of the kingdom of God, one must have a clear sense of one's own beliefs in relation to the branch of theology known as eschatology, which deals with the "last things" or "end times." In today's religious marketplace, one encounters a variety of eschatologies—from literalist beliefs influenced by the *Left Behind* series (best-selling novels published 1995-2007) that deal with the end, to the Social Gospel's vision of building the kingdom of God on earth by enlightened human effort within history. I try to adhere to what I understand to be the Church's traditional teachings, while acknowledging that the scriptures speak on these matters in highly symbolic language and poetic imagery of realities that can hardly otherwise be described at all. For those wishing to pursue these crucially important theological issues further, I recommend *The Oxford Handbook of Eschatology* (2010) edited by Jerry Walls.

Ultimately, the seasons of Advent, Christmas, and Epiphany point in converging lines to the Word-made-flesh, Jesus Christ, the incarnate Son of God. His first coming two thousand years ago made the kingdom of God a reality within history, yet still a reality that awaits his return for its final fulfillment and consummation. My hope is that these homilies will bring the reader to contemplate more closely this great mystery and its promise of salvation and new life for all creation.

The First Sunday of Advent

YEAR A	YEAR B	YEAR C
Isaiah 2:1-5	Isaiah 64:1-9	Jeremiah 33:14-16
Psalm 122	Psalm 80:1-7, 16-18	Psalm 25:1-9
Romans 13:11-14	1 Corinthians 1:3-9	1 Thessalonians 3:9-13
Matthew 24:36-44	Mark 13:24-37	Luke 21:25-36

The eucharistic readings for the First Sunday of Advent (Years A, B, and C) begin a new liturgical year by announcing the biblical expectation of the kingdom of God. The readings from the Hebrew scriptures envision the nations of the earth coming to worship the Lord in Jerusalem, and the reign of God's messiah, a descendent of King David who will execute justice and righteousness in the land. The psalms express joy at this prospect, combined with poignant longing. The epistle readings highlight the need to be prepared for the return of Christ on the Last Day, combined with assurances that God equips us with the grace necessary to be ready. Significantly, the gospel readings for all three years are taken from the discourse of Jesus known as the "Little

Apocalypse" (Matthew 24-25; Mark 13; Luke 21:5-36). These readings combine several interlocking motifs: the glorious return of the Son of Man, the need to read the signs of the times to discern when the time is near, the impossibility of predicting the exact day and hour, and the consequent need to watch, pray, and be prepared at all times.

The readings on the weekdays expand and develop various aspects of this biblical hope. They afford glimpses of the kingdom from various perspectives.

Monday in 1 Advent

The Gathering of the Nations
Isaiah 2:1-5 (or in Year A, Isaiah 4:2-6)
Psalm 122
Matthew 8:5-13

*(Note: Today's Old Testament reading and psalm
are the same as on the First Sunday of Advent, Year A.)*

The season of Advent calls us to reexamine our attitudes as Christians toward time: past, present, and future. We often classify people's basic orientation to time into two broad categories: optimism and pessimism.

Optimists believe that things are getting better. For them the past is full of bad things—wars, famines, epidemics, tyranny, ignorance, and superstition—that humanity is gradually overcoming by the progress of reason, education, science, technology, and medicine. For optimists, the future is attractive and exciting; it holds the promise of peace, prosperity, long life, and happiness.

Pessimists believe, on the contrary, that things are getting worse. They look back to earlier decades of their lives—or perhaps to earlier centuries of history they've read about in books—a golden age that will never return. For pessimists, the present is marked by corruption and decay portending future disaster, whether in the form of rising crime rates or rising ocean levels.

The biblical orientation to time combines pessimism and optimism in a unique way. During this season, many of the readings we hear in church belong to the genre called apocalyptic.

Apocalyptic thought discerns a unique pattern to history. In the present, all is not right with the world; God's people are subject to trials and tribulations inflicted by the evil powers that control the present age. Things are going to get worse before they get better. In this sense, apocalyptic embodies a decidedly pessimistic outlook.

Eventually, however, the troubles of the present age will escalate to a point of crisis when God will intervene in history to defeat the powers of evil and to usher in a whole new state of affairs, referred to in biblical shorthand as the kingdom (or reign) of God. Biblical descriptions of the kingdom of God portray in vivid imagery a time of unparalleled peace, happiness, and fulfillment for all humanity—indeed for the entire cosmos. In this sense, apocalyptic embodies a supremely optimistic outlook. But its optimism is based not on faith in inevitable human progress but rather on hope in God's promises.

During this first week of Advent, the daily eucharistic readings invite us to contemplate God's future through descriptions of God's kingdom found in the Bible. Many of these depictions are couched in highly symbolic imagery that should not be taken literally but that point to sublime and mysterious realities otherwise impossible to describe.

Today's readings highlight one key feature of the kingdom of God: it will include all nations and peoples of the earth, not just one nation or one people. Hence the reading from Isaiah depicts all the nations coming to worship at "the mountain of the Lord's house"—that is, the temple mount in Jerusalem—in a reign of universal peace where "they shall beat their swords into plowshares, and their spears into pruning hooks." Psalm 122 echoes the joy of "the tribes of the Lord" going up to worship in Jerusalem. And in the reading from Matthew, in response to the faith of a Roman centurion, Jesus promises, "many will come from east and west and will eat with Abraham and Isaac and Jacob in the kingdom of heaven."

In biblical times, worshiping in the temple and eating together were activities in which Jews maintained a strict separation from Gentiles. Only Jews were allowed into the inner courts of the temple, and Jews incurred ritual defilement and impurity by eating with Gentiles.

We human beings have erected all sorts of barriers among ourselves according to distinctions of race, class, nationality, gender, ethnicity, and ideology. In the Church, we are called to do all we can to overcome such barriers, both within our own communities and in the wider society. Today's readings offer the promise of a future in which all such divisions will be no more, and all people of all backgrounds will worship God and feast together in the banquet of God's kingdom.

Tuesday in 1 Advent

The Coming of the Messiah

Isaiah 11:1-10
Psalm 72:1-8
Luke 10:21-24

(Note: Today's Old Testament reading and psalm are also appointed for the Second Sunday of Advent, Year A.)

A kingdom requires a king. On the basis of numerous prophecies in the Hebrew scriptures, the people of Israel were expecting a king, the messiah, who would be the human agent of God's reign on earth.

In Old Testament times, people understood today's readings from Isaiah and the Psalms to be prophecies of the messiah. "A shoot shall come out from the stump of Jesse, and a branch shall grow out of the roots." That is, the messiah would be descended from King David, the son of Jesse. Even in a time when the Davidic monarchy seemed to have been cut off, a descendant of David would arise to inaugurate God's kingdom.

The reading from Isaiah makes clear that this messiah would rule not by human power, but in the Spirit of the Lord: "the spirit of wisdom and understanding, the spirit of counsel and might, the spirit of the knowledge and fear of the Lord." For this reason alone, true justice and righteousness would characterize his reign. And the prophet describes the effects of his reign, extending even to the transformation of relationships between predators and prey in the natural world:

> *The wolf shall live with the lamb,*
> *and the leopard shall lie down with the kid,*
> *the calf and the lion and the fatling together,*
> *and a little child shall lead them.*

Psalm 72 similarly describes the messiah's universal and everlasting reign of justice and peace:

> *He shall defend the needy among the people;*
> > *he shall rescue the poor and crush the oppressor.*
> *He shall live as long as the sun and moon*
> > *endure, from one generation to another…*
> *In his time shall the righteous flourish;*
> > *there shall be abundance of peace till the moon shall be no more.*
> *He shall rule from sea to sea,*
> > *and from the River to the ends of the earth.*

Advent, it has been said, invites the Church to re-identify itself with Israel waiting for the messiah. As Christians, we are called during this season to experience for ourselves Israel's longing, hope, and anticipation for the promised king.

Yet we also believe that he has already come. The Hebrew word *messiah* literally means "anointed one." Translated into Greek, it becomes *christos*, or "Christ." So, when the Church added the title "Christ" to the name of Jesus, it was explicitly proclaiming that Jesus is the messiah of Jewish expectation.

In today's gospel, Jesus himself makes this affirmation. Speaking privately to his disciples, he declares: "Blessed are the eyes that see what you see! For I tell you that many prophets and kings desired to see what you see, but did not see it, and to hear what you hear, but did not hear it."

The Latin word "advent" means arrival or coming. During this season, it has become traditional to speak of two—or in some cases, three—comings of the Lord. As Christians, we believe that the messiah has already come in the person of Jesus of Nazareth, the incarnate Son of God. That is his first coming.

In a way that is impossible to describe ahead of time in anything but symbolic (and poetic) language, he will come again at the end of the present age, to judge the living and the dead and to inaugurate the reign of God over the entire cosmos. That is his second coming.

Some traditions of Christian spirituality also speak of a "third coming" of the Lord into our hearts, here and now. Certainly the season of Advent calls us to be awake and alert, ready to welcome him whenever he comes.

So, as Israel awaits the coming of the messiah, Christians await Christ's return. The Old Testament readings and psalms for Advent unite us in joyful longing and hope for the bearer of God's universal reign.

Wednesday in 1 Advent

The Messianic Banquet
Isaiah 25:6-9
Psalm 23
Matthew 15:29-39

Eating and drinking are among the most basic human activities. Food and drink are necessary to our physical survival. In almost all cultures, moreover, we ideally eat and drink together. Shared meals forge and strengthen the bonds of friendship, conviviality, and community.

It should not be surprising, then, that biblical descriptions of the kingdom of God often include images of feasting. A recurring motif is the messianic banquet. A basic principle of Christian theology is that life in the world to come will not negate, but rather fulfill, the best features of life in this world.

Today's readings develop this theme in various ways. In the reading from Isaiah, the prophet foretells, "On this mountain [Mount Zion in Jerusalem] the LORD of hosts will make for all peoples a feast of rich food, a feast of well-aged wines, of rich food filled with marrow, of well-aged wines strained clear."

In this meditation on the Lord caring for people as a shepherd cares for sheep in the midst of danger, Psalm 23 introduces the motif of being fed:

> *You spread a table before me in the presence*
>   *of those who trouble me;*
> *you have anointed my head with oil,*
>   *and my cup is running over.*

Early Christian commentators related this verse to baptism and the eucharist. In the early Church, new converts were anointed with oil immediately following baptism. Then, as they proceeded into the place where the eucharist was to be celebrated, they sang Psalm 23, understanding the "table" and the "cup" as those from which they were about to receive communion for the first time. They had also been taught that the eucharistic meal itself was not only a present sharing in the sacramental Body and Blood of Christ, but also a foretaste of the messianic banquet in the kingdom of God.

This background helps put into perspective the significance of today's gospel of the feeding of the four thousand. The miraculous multiplication of the loaves and fish in the wilderness echoes the Old Testament prophecies of superabundant quantities of food and drink in the kingdom of God. The story thus makes the point that Jesus is the Messiah, the bearer of God's kingdom.

At the same time, miraculous as it is, the event points beyond itself to even greater realities. Matthew's depiction of Jesus' actions—taking, giving thanks, breaking, and distributing—seems consciously to anticipate his actions at the Last Supper, which are carried forward into the Holy Eucharist.

Today's scripture readings offer us, then, a glimpse of the messianic banquet. Whenever we gather as the Church to celebrate the eucharist, we receive an anticipatory foretaste of that great feast.

Thursday in 1 Advent

An Everlasting Rock
Isaiah 26:1-6
Psalm 118:19-24
Matthew 7:21-27

Protection against attacking armies and marauding invaders in the ancient world depended on cities with strong walls. A city built on rocky heights commanding the surrounding countryside generally afforded the greatest security of all. At the approach of a hostile foe, the inhabitants of the region would stream in through the gates to take refuge; the gates would then be closed to repulse the enemy.

Today's readings introduce a note of tension and conflict to the Advent hope of God's kingdom. Images of gates in walled cities built on foundations of rock imply that before the kingdom comes, God's people will be subject to conflicts, tumults, and storms against which only God can provide a sure defense.

Humanly fortified cities provide no absolute guarantee of protection. In the Old Testament reading, the prophet Isaiah warns that God casts down those who proudly trust in fortifications of their own devising: "He has brought low the inhabitants of the height; the lofty city he lays low. He lays it low to the ground, casts it to the dust."

At the same time, the prophet proclaims that "on that day"—that is, on the Day of the Lord, when the kingdom of God arrives—the inhabitants of Judah will sing, "We have a strong city." Its gates will be opened so that "the righteous nation that keeps faith may enter in." This city, moreover, is built on the rock of trust in God: "for in the Lord God you have an everlasting rock." The underlying theme is one of reversal: the city built on human pride is cast down from the heights; a new strong city built on trust in God is raised up in its place.

Psalm 118 echoes these themes. The psalmist sings of ascending Mount Zion to worship in the temple. On the way up, the pilgrims must pass through the gates of Jerusalem, and again through the gates of the temple precincts: "Open for me the gates of righteousness; I will enter through them; I will offer thanks to the Lord."

Then the psalmist sounds a mysterious note of reversal: "The same stone which the builders rejected has become the chief cornerstone. This is the Lord's doing, and it is marvelous in our eyes." It is not entirely clear what these verses meant in their original context. Beginning with certain sayings of Jesus in the gospels, however, the early

Christians understood them to refer to one rejected by the leaders of the people (Jesus himself) being vindicated by God (in the Resurrection) to become the cornerstone of a new spiritual edifice (the Church).

Finally, in today's gospel, Jesus tells a parable of two houses, one built on rock and one built on sand. The one who hears the words of Jesus and acts upon them is like a wise man who builds his house on rock. Conversely, the one who hears these words and does not respond to them is like a foolish man who builds his house on sand. The rains, floods, and wind that assault each house are the tribulations that precede the Day of the Lord in apocalyptic thought. The house built on the rock of obedience to the Lord's teachings stands; the house built on the sands of human disobedience and self-will is washed away.

Today's readings subtly introduce the idea of judgment as an integral component of the Advent theme of anticipating God's kingdom. The good news is that the kingdom of God is like a strong city built on rock. But not necessarily everyone can enter in through its gates. As Jesus himself puts it: "Not everyone who says to me, 'Lord, Lord,' will enter the kingdom of heaven, but only the one who does the will of my Father in heaven." How we best prepare ourselves to face this judgment is a continuing concern of the scripture readings throughout the Advent season.

Friday in 1 Advent

The Beatific Vision
Isaiah 29:17-24
Psalm 26:1-6, 17-18
Matthew 9:27-31

Of all our senses, we normally rely most on sight and hearing for information about the world around us. To be aware of our surroundings, we need first to look and listen. Our other senses—taste, touch, and smell—tell us much as well, from scents of telltale odors and fragrances in our nostrils, to cold drops of rain on our skin. But for most of us, seeing and hearing are primary.

From time immemorial, blindness and deafness have been considered particularly cruel ailments. Although blind and deaf people learn to compensate for their conditions in remarkable ways—including amazing development of the acuity of their other senses—the loss of sight or hearing always presents a formidable challenge.

Against this background, today's readings suggest two important points. First, seeing and hearing help us not only to be aware of our natural and earthly surroundings but also help us to grasp God's truth and to behold God's beauty. Second, in the kingdom of God, there will be no more blindness or deafness; those who are blind and deaf in this world will have their sight and hearing restored.

"On that day," the prophet Isaiah declares, "the deaf shall hear the words of a scroll, and out of their gloom and darkness the eyes of the blind shall see." The "words of a scroll" allude to the words of scripture. The prophet is declaring not only the blessing of restored hearing, but also a recovered ability to hear and understand the word of the Lord.

Psalm 27 similarly links seeing to the ability to encounter God in the context of worship:

> *One thing have I asked of the LORD; one thing I seek;*
> *that I may dwell in the house of the LORD all the days of*
> *my life;*
> *To behold the fair beauty of the LORD;*
> *and to seek him in his temple* (Psalm 27:5-6).

On the basis of this and similar texts, certain streams of Christian spirituality have named the blessedness enjoyed by the saints in heaven "the beatific vision"—seeing God face to face, beholding the fair beauty of the Lord.

Jesus' miracles of restoring hearing to the deaf and sight to the blind—as we encounter in today's gospel—have a triple significance.

First, they are deeds of mercy and compassion in and of themselves. Those who regain their hearing or sight are enabled to participate in the life and work of the community in a way that was previously impossible for them.

Second, they point beyond themselves to the kingdom of God, where all hearing and sight will be restored to the deaf and the blind, so that all people may hear God's words and "behold the fair beauty of the Lord."

Third, they remind us that deafness and blindness can be spiritual as well as physical. Even those who have physical sight and hearing can be deaf to the voice of conscience and blind to the things of the spirit.

Today's readings call our attention to the restoration of sight to the blind and hearing to the deaf as definitive signs of the coming of God's kingdom. During this season of Advent, we do well to pray that God will open our eyes and unstop our ears as well.

Saturday in 1 Advent

Healing Every Disease and Every Infirmity
Isaiah 30:19-21, 23-26
Psalm 147:1-12
Matthew 9:35-10:1, 5-8

The human spirit protests against sickness and disease. At a deep level of our being, we regard illness, infirmity, and injury as signs that all is not right with the world, things are not as they should be.

Hope for the restoration of humanity to right relationship with God unavoidably includes hope for healing of our ailments: physical, moral, and spiritual. Conversely, when healing occurs—whether by means of medical science or means that seem and may indeed be supernatural—we sense God's presence and grace at work in our midst.

Today's readings call our attention to healing as a sign of the coming of God's kingdom. The psalmist proclaims:

> *The Lord rebuilds Jerusalem;*
> > *he gathers the exiles of Israel.*
> *He heals the brokenhearted and binds up their wounds.*

The prophet Isaiah similarly foretells a day when "the Lord binds up the injuries of his people, and heals the wounds inflicted by his blow." This verse reflects the prophet's belief that God has permitted the people to suffer as punishment for their sins—in order to correct and educate them so that they might ultimately be restored to their favored position, their injuries bound up and their wounds healed.

Healing was one of the signature activities of Jesus. Today's gospel reading captures the flavor of his ministry in Galilee: "Then Jesus went about all the cities and villages, teaching in their synagogues, and proclaiming the good news of the kingdom, and curing every disease and every sickness."

Then, commissioning the twelve apostles, he gives them a share in his authority: "As you go, proclaim the good news, 'The kingdom of heaven has come near.' Cure the sick, raise the dead, cleanse the lepers, cast out demons."

The point to note in both instances is the linking of healing to the proclamation of the good news of the kingdom of God. By his miraculous healings, Jesus enacts the fulfillment of Old Testament prophecies, demonstrating that the kingdom is already present in and through his ministry. At the same time, however, this ministry of healing points beyond itself to the coming of the kingdom in its fullness upon his return, which still remains in the future.

In this life, our physical ailments subliminally remind us that we inhabit mortal bodies subject to inevitable decay, disintegration, and death. Rather than stoically accepting this fate, however, we long for ultimate restoration and wholeness—indeed, for eternal life.

The good news of the kingdom includes the promise that in the world to come all of our afflictions in this life—physical, mental, emotional, and spiritual—will indeed be healed. The doctrine of the Resurrection assures us that beyond physical decay and death, God is preparing a new body for us to inhabit a world made new.

The Second Sunday of Advent

YEAR A	YEAR B	YEAR C
Isaiah 11:1-10	Isaiah 40:1-11	Baruch 5:1-9 or
Psalm 72:1-7, 18-19	Psalm 85:1-2, 8-13	Malachi 3:1-4
Romans 15:4-13	2 Peter 3:8-15a	Canticle 4 or 16
Matthew 3:1-12	Mark 1:1-8	Philippians 1:3-11
		Luke 3:1-6

The three parallel gospel readings appointed for the Second Sunday of Advent introduce the figure of John the Baptist as foretold in Isaiah 40:3, "The voice of one crying out in the wilderness: Prepare the way of the Lord, make his paths straight!" All three gospels describe John's ministry of preaching and administering a baptism of repentance for the forgiveness of sins. Matthew (Year A) includes John's warnings to the Pharisees and Sadducees to "bear fruit that befits repentance." Matthew (Year A) and Mark (Year B) describe John's distinctive garments and diet: clothed with camels' hair and a leather belt around his waist, eating locusts and wild honey. They also include his proclamation of one more powerful coming after him who will baptize with the Holy Spirit. Luke (Year C) distinctively identifies the precise time and political situation in history when John appeared: "In the fifteenth year of the reign of the Emperor Tiberias, when Pontius Pilate was governor of Judea, and Herod was ruler of Galilee…during the high priesthood of Annas and Caiaphas…"

The eucharistic readings appointed for the weekdays following develop and explore themes associated with John's ministry and proclamation.

Monday in 2 Advent

A Highway in the Desert
Isaiah 35:1-10
Psalm 85:8-13
Luke 5:17-26

(Note: Today's Old Testament reading is also appointed for the Third Sunday of Advent, Year A, and Proper 18, Year B.)

Yesterday, the gospel readings for the Second Sunday of Advent introduced the figure of Saint John the Baptist. Today's readings do not mention John but are nonetheless dominated by themes associated with his ministry.

The reading from Isaiah 35 features a highway in the wilderness, "the Holy Way," over which "the ransomed of the Lord shall return, and come to Zion with singing." This image is closely related to that in Isaiah 40:3: "A voice cries out: 'In the wilderness prepare the way of the Lord; make straight in the desert a highway for our God'" This is in turn quoted by all three gospel readings for the Second Sunday of Advent in relation to John the Baptist.

Today's gospel addresses Jesus' authority to forgive sins; and all three years' gospel readings for the Second

Sunday of Advent describe John preaching "a baptism of repentance for the forgiveness of sins." This theme of forgiveness is also at least implied in Psalm 85:8: "I will listen to what the Lord God is saying, for he is speaking peace to his faithful people and to those who turn their hearts to him."

So, today's readings invoke two themes associated with John the Baptist: a highway in the desert, and the forgiveness of sins. The biblical background of both themes is the Babylonian captivity.

In the year 587 BCE, the forces of the Babylonian empire destroyed Jerusalem, including the temple, and took the king and all the leading citizens of the kingdom of Judah into exile in Babylon. Much of what we know today as the Old Testament was edited in its final form during the fifty-year period of exile that followed (although many of its writings are much older).

The question that dominated the minds of the exiles was why God had allowed such a catastrophe to happen—he had promised that King David's throne and kingdom would last forever. Was God unfaithful? Or was God no match for the gods of Babylon? The exiles gradually discerned that the truth was that Israel had been unfaithful to its covenant with God, and the exile was God's just punishment for the people's sins.

Eventually, about the year 538 BCE, the Persians conquered Babylon and allowed the exiles to return to Judah and rebuild the temple. Sometime shortly before the return, there appeared among the exiles a prophet (or prophets) whose writings are recorded in chapters 40 through 55 of the Book of Isaiah. (Some scholars think that chapters 34 and 35 also date from this period.) Conveniently known as "Second Isaiah," this prophet announced in a series of exquisitely beautiful oracles the imminent return of the people—and their God—to Jerusalem.

A key theme of Second Isaiah is that the people's sins are forgiven; they have paid double for the transgressions for which the exile was punishment:

Comfort, O comfort my people, says your God.
Speak tenderly to Jerusalem, and cry to her
   that she has served her term,
   that her penalty is paid,
that she has received from the LORD's hand
   double for all her sins. (Isaiah 40:1-2)

Immediately following this announcement of forgiveness, the prophet proclaims: "In the wilderness prepare the way of the LORD, make straight in the desert a highway for our God" (Isaiah 40:3). The highway is envisioned as a road across the desert from Babylon back to Jerusalem, over which God will lead God's people home. The image of the highway thus speaks of liberation, return from exile, and homecoming, which in turn signifies God's forgiveness of the people's sins.

How does this background illuminate the ministry of John the Baptist? Biblical scholar N.T. Wright has argued that in New Testament times the Jewish people saw their life under Roman occupation as a continuing state of exile in their own land.

By invoking the words of Isaiah, "In the wilderness prepare the way of the Lord," and preaching a baptism of repentance for the forgiveness of sins, John the Baptist was in effect announcing the end of exile and the imminent coming of God to inaugurate the kingdom—themes to be explored further in the days that follow.

Tuesday in 2 Advent

Offer to God a Sacrifice of Thanksgiving

Isaiah 40:1-11 (or in Year B, Amos 5:18-24)
Psalm 96 (or in Year B, Psalm 50:7-15)
Matthew 18:12-14

(Note: Isaiah 40:1-11 is the Old Testament reading on the Second Sunday of Advent, Year B. Amos 5:18-24 is also appointed for Proper 23, Year B. This homily uses the Year B readings.)

The message of John the Baptist is not only "good news" (Luke 3:18) but also a profound challenge. The kingdom is coming, yes, but the people must prepare to enter it by the way of repentance. Hence John administers a baptism of repentance for the forgiveness of sins: "Then the people of Jerusalem and all Judea were going out to him, and all the region along the Jordan, and they were baptized by him in the river Jordan, confessing their sins" (Matthew 3:5-6).

But when John sees Pharisees and Sadducees—the religious elite—coming for baptism, he speaks harsh words, warning them of impending judgment and destruction:

You brood of vipers! Who warned you to flee from the wrath to come? Bear fruit worthy of repentance. Do not presume to say to yourselves, "We have Abraham as our ancestor"; for I tell you, God is able from these stones to raise up children to Abraham. Even now the ax is lying at the root of the trees; every tree therefore that does not bear good fruit is cut down and thrown into the fire (Matthew 3:7b-10).

In this passage, heard on the Second Sunday of Advent in Year A, John the Baptist warns the Pharisees and Sadducees against presuming that their descent from Abraham, and hence their membership in God's chosen people, will suffice to spare them from the wrath about to come upon the world. They must repent of their sins, for already the ax is poised to strike down every tree that does not bear good fruit.

John is speaking in the classical tradition of Old Testament prophecy, exemplified in today's reading from the Book of Amos. Prophesying in the eighth century BCE at the northern kingdom's royal shrine at Bethel, Amos warns his listeners that despite their desire for the Day of the Lord when the Lord comes to inaugurate his kingdom, this will be for them a day of judgment and condemnation: "It is darkness, not light; as if someone fled from a lion, and was met by a bear; or went into the house and rested a hand against the wall, and was bitten by a snake."

Amos then identifies the people's chief sin as complacency: resting content in the outward ceremonial observances of religion while structuring a society with systematic injustice and oppression. Speaking in the name of God, the prophet denounces the people's hypocritical practice of religion:

> *I hate, I despise your festivals,*
> > *and I take no delight in your solemn assemblies.*
>
> *Even though you offer me your burnt offerings and*
> > *grain offerings,*
>
> *I will not accept them;*
> > *and the offerings of well-being of your fatted*
> > *animals I will not look upon.*
>
> *Take away from me the noise of your songs;*
> > *I will not listen to the melody of your harps.*
>
> *But let justice roll down like waters,*
> > *and righteousness like an ever-flowing stream*
> > (Amos 5:21-24).

Psalm 50 echoes similar themes. The people's sacrifices of bulls and goats in the temple are all well and good, but ultimately God wants something more: "Offer to God a sacrifice of thanksgiving and make good your vows to the Most High."

Centuries later, John the Baptist warns the Pharisees and Sadducees to bear fruit worthy of repentance and not to rely on their Abrahamic descent for entrance into God's kingdom, much as Amos warned the inhabitants of Bethel not to rely on religious observances alone without practicing justice and righteousness.

Today's gospel about the lost sheep puts all these prophetic denunciations and warnings into proper perspective. By sending the prophets, up through and including John the Baptist, God is searching for and seeking out the lost. The purpose of prophecy is not to gloat over the punishment awaiting unrepentant sinners but to call those sinners to repentance so that the punishment won't be necessary. Just so, Jesus tells us, a shepherd having lost one out of a hundred sheep seeks out the one that has gone astray, and on finding the lost sheep rejoices over it more than over the ninety-nine who never went astray.

Wednesday in 2 Advent

You Will Find Rest for Your Souls
Isaiah 40:25-31
Psalm 103:1-10
Matthew 11:28-30

In 1902 the satirist Finley Peter Dunne coined the phrase "Comfort the afflicted and afflict the comfortable." On the lips of his protagonist Mr. Dooley, the saying had no explicitly religious import. It was intended as a description of the work of newspapers to expose corruption in high places and bring to public awareness the sufferings of victims of political and economic oppression.

Cosmo Gordon Lang, Archbishop of Canterbury from 1928 to 1942, appropriated the phrase in relation to the work of the Church, often describing it as the supreme goal of religion. It also became associated with Henry Wise Hobson, Bishop of Southern Ohio from 1938 to 1959, and was the title of a Forward Movement biography of Bishop Hobson by Robert R. Hansel in 1982.

Certainly, the saying expresses a key theme in biblical theology. Many of the discourses, speeches, letters, and sayings in the Bible, including those of the prophets, John the Baptist, and Jesus himself, seem intended either to afflict the comfortable or to comfort the afflicted. Today's readings fall exclusively into the latter category. In the context of the Advent season, they remind us that the promise of God's kingdom is indeed comfort for the afflicted.

The Old Testament reading from Isaiah describes God strengthening the weak and powerless who wait for the Lord:

> *He gives power to the faint,*
> *   and strengthens the powerless.*
> *Even youths will faint and be weary,*
> *   and the young will fall exhausted;*
> *but those who wait for the Lord shall renew*
> *   their strength,*
> *   they shall mount up with wings like eagles,*
> *   they shall run and not be weary,*
> *   they shall walk and not faint* (Isaiah 40:29-31).

The word "faint," which occurs three times in this passage, is often used in the Old Testament to describe those who faint from hunger and thirst. More pointedly, it also describes those who lose courage at the power of their enemies. This passage comforts those who, in the present age, are faint and weary. When the Lord comes and liberates them from their oppressors, they "shall mount up with wings like eagles," no longer exhausted or powerless, but full of strength and courage.

Psalm 103 reads as a litany of comfort, enumerating God's saving deeds—forgiving iniquity, healing diseases, bringing life from death. Significantly, like the reading from Isaiah, it also makes use of the image of an eagle: "[The Lord] satisfies you with good things, and your youth is renewed like an eagle's."

In today's short gospel reading, Jesus issues his beloved invitation: "Come to me, all you that are weary and are carrying heavy burdens, and I will give you rest." Here the image of rest evokes the sabbath, the seventh day, when God rested from all the works of creation and commanded all to abstain from work and labor. The early Christians understood the Jewish sabbath as a symbolic weekly anticipation of the final rest of the kingdom of God when all creation would have eternal leisure to rest, worship, celebrate, and enjoy God's presence.

Jesus continues: "Take my yoke upon you and learn from me; for I am gentle and humble in heart, and you will find rest for your souls. For my yoke is easy, and my burden is light."

In much of the Bible, yokes and burdens signify servitude, and especially political domination. In New Testament times, the Jews complained of the yoke of Roman rule. Here, Jesus contrasts himself with the oppressive rulers and taskmasters of the present age. Their yokes are difficult and their burdens are heavy. But to follow Jesus is to accept an easy yoke and a light burden. This message is comfort for the afflicted. Following Jesus in this life brings rest for our souls, pointing to the perfect rest in the world to come.

Thursday in 2 Advent

A Prophet, and More Than a Prophet

Isaiah 41:13-20
Psalm 145:1-4, 8-13
Matthew 11:7-15

Starting today, John the Baptist figures explicitly in the weekday gospel readings. On Sunday the readings were taken from the beginning sections of one of the three synoptic gospels (Matthew, Mark, and Luke), describing John's ministry of preaching and baptizing at the River Jordan. Today's gospel is taken from a subsequent section of Matthew set at the time after John has been imprisoned. Here Jesus reflects on the significance of John's ministry as the forerunner.

In the episode immediately preceding today's gospel, John has sent word to Jesus from prison, asking, "Are you the one who is to come, or are we to wait for another?" The question betrays a surprising degree of uncertainty on John's part given his earlier testimony at the time of Jesus' baptism. Perhaps John is expecting a different kind of messiah than Jesus is turning out to be: specifically a messiah who will lead a military rebellion against Roman rule (and against the tyrant king Herod Antipas who has imprisoned John), and who will thus liberate John from prison.

In this case, Jesus' answer not only implicitly affirms that he is indeed the Messiah, "the one who is to come," but also clarifies what kind of messiah he is. "Go and tell John what you hear and see: the blind receive their sight and the lame walk, lepers are cleansed and the deaf hear, and the dead are raised up, and the poor have good news preached to them." In other words, Jesus' ministry of preaching, healing, and performing miracles fulfills the Old Testament prophecies, particularly those found in the prophet Isaiah.

Once the messengers have departed, today's gospel begins with Jesus addressing the crowds concerning John. They went out into the wilderness to see neither "a reed shaken by the wind" (Jesus here may be alluding to the tall grasses on the banks of the Jordan), nor "someone dressed in soft robes" (Jesus here may be alluding to King Herod Antipas himself, who lived in a fortress in the wilderness). Instead, John was a prophet, "and more than a prophet."

To explain what he means by "more than a prophet," Jesus refers to a prophecy from the Old Testament Book of Malachi, "See, I am sending my messenger to prepare the way before me…" (Malachi 3:1). John was not only a prophet but also the forerunner, the messenger sent to prepare the way for the messiah, Jesus.

Jesus then speaks the words: "Truly I tell you, among those born of women no one has arisen greater than John the Baptist; yet the least in the kingdom of heaven is greater than he." That is, John is the last and greatest of the prophets, but even so, he is only the forerunner of something much greater, namely the kingdom of God. John belongs to the present age, but a new age is dawning in which even the least occupy a position of infinitely greater privilege and blessing.

The next sentence has baffled many commentators: "From the days of John the Baptist until now the kingdom of heaven has suffered violence, and the violent take it by force." It is not entirely clear what Jesus means by the kingdom of heaven having suffered violence, or who the men of violence are who take it by force. A possible meaning is that as an agent or representative of the kingdom, John has suffered imprisonment and will soon be beheaded—just as Jesus will ultimately suffer arrest, trial, condemnation, and crucifixion. But some interpreters think that this reading conflicts with the previous statement's implication that John is outside the kingdom. All in all, the precise meaning of the saying remains obscure.

Jesus then mysteriously identifies John with "Elijah who is to come." The allusion is to Malachi 4:5: "Lo, I will send you the prophet Elijah before the great and terrible day of the Lord comes." As recounted in 2 Kings 2:11-12, Elijah did not die but was taken up into heaven by a chariot of fire and horses of fire. On the basis of the prophecy in Malachi, many Jews expected the return of Elijah from heaven as the sign of the imminent arrival of God's kingdom. (To this day at the Passover Seder, observant Jews pour a cup of wine for Elijah in case he shows up.) As will become clear in the days to come, however, Jesus did not identify John the Baptist with a literally returned Elijah, but rather as what might be called "an Elijah figure" or one exercising the office of Elijah as the forerunner of God's Kingdom.

In today's gospel Jesus clarifies the relationship between John the Baptist and himself—not least for the benefit of John's followers who must soon decide how they will relate to Jesus, his disciples, and ultimately the Christian Church. Jesus is "the one who is to come," the Messiah, the bearer of God's kingdom. Yet Jesus affirms John's ministry as that of the messenger sent before him to prepare his way, and as Elijah, whose appearance heralds the Day of the Lord.

Friday in 2 Advent

Wisdom is Vindicated by Her Deeds
Isaiah 48:17-19
Psalm 1
Matthew 11:16-19

During this Advent season so far, we have encountered various Old Testament prophecies of the coming of God's kingdom. In the gospels we have seen how these prophecies begin to find fulfillment in the earthly life and ministry of Jesus of Nazareth. This fulfillment awaits its final completion when the risen and ascended Christ returns at the end of the present world to judge the living and the dead. Today's readings introduce the possibility that some will reject and resist this prophetic message. In the reading from Isaiah, God (speaking through the prophet) laments:

> *O that you had paid attention to my commandments!*
> *Then your prosperity would have been like a river, and*
>   *your success like the waves of the sea;*
> *your offspring would have been like the sand,*
>   *and your descendants like its grains;*
> *their name would never be cut off or destroyed from*
>   *before me.*

Drawing a contrast between the way of the righteous and the way of the wicked, Psalm 1 warns, "the wicked shall not stand upright when judgment comes, nor the sinner in the council of the righteous."

The call to prepare for the coming of the kingdom is good news, but not everyone is willing to receive it. In today's gospel, Jesus contrasts the nearly opposite ways in which he and John the Baptist have delivered almost the same message, only to meet with widespread criticism and rejection.

Alluding to what may have been a familiar children's song, Jesus likens the present generation to children in the marketplaces calling to one another: "We played the flute for you, and you did not dance; we wailed, and you did not mourn."

In the same way, Jesus continues, John the Baptist came practicing a severe ascetic lifestyle, "neither eating nor drinking," and they say, "He has a demon." But then the Son of Man came in a celebratory mode, eating and drinking, and they say, "Look, a glutton and a drunkard, a friend of tax collectors and sinners!"

Most commentators interpret the phrase, "we played the flute for you, and you did not dance" as figuratively addressed by Jesus to those who rejected him because of his table fellowship with disreputable members of society. Similarly, John figuratively addresses the words "we wailed, and you did not mourn" to those who have rejected him for his ascetic lifestyle and his call to repentance and baptism.

Another interpretation notes, however, that it is "this generation" that is compared to the children in the marketplaces. According to this reading, those who wanted John to adopt a more celebratory and festive lifestyle are the ones who speak to him the words "we played the flute for you, and you did not dance," while those who wanted Jesus to adopt a more ascetic lifestyle, as well as a sterner and harsher posture towards sinners, are the ones who reproach him with the words, "we wailed, and you did not mourn."

Either way, the point is that despite the very different approaches of John the Baptist and Jesus, not everyone has been willing or able to receive their message. Those who preach good news from God should not be surprised to encounter hostility and rejection.

"Yet," Jesus adds, "wisdom is vindicated by her deeds." This proverbial saying suggests that the words and actions of both John the Baptist and Jesus reflect and express a deeper wisdom from God. Despite many people's rejection of both John and Jesus, their ministries are unfolding according to a hidden divine plan in which apparent defeat turns out to be victory in disguise.

Saturday in 2 Advent

Elijah Has Already Come
Sirach 48:1-11
Psalm 80:1-3, 14-18
Matthew 17:9-13

Today's readings continue to explore the identification of John the Baptist with the prophet Elijah. The reading from the apocryphal Book of Wisdom (also known as Sirach) consists of a hymn singing Elijah's praises and recounting his spectacular deeds. Of particular interest are verses 9 and 10:

> *You were taken up by a whirlwind of fire,*
> *in a chariot with horses of fire.*
> *At the appointed time, it is written,*
> *you are destined to calm the wrath of God before it*
> *breaks out in fury,*
> *to turn the hearts of parents to their children,*
> *and to restore the tribes of Jacob.*

These verses hark back to the prophecy in the Book of Malachi: "Lo, I will send you the prophet Elijah before the great and terrible day of the Lord comes. He will turn the hearts of parents to their children and the hearts of children to their parents, so that I will not come and strike the land with a curse." (Malachi 4:5-6)

Already, we can see a correspondence between this description of Elijah's return and John the Baptist's understanding of his own ministry. The returned Elijah will mitigate God's wrath on the Day of the Lord by turning the hearts of parents to their children and the hearts of children to their parents. This reconciliation between generations implies reconciliation between all those at enmity with one another and, in the widest possible sense, repentance from sin in general.

John the Baptist clearly saw his mission in such terms. He based his call to repentance on the expectation of God's wrath about to be let loose upon a fallen and sinful world: "You brood of vipers! Who warned you to flee from the wrath to come?" By repenting of their sins and receiving John's baptism, God's people had the opportunity to prepare themselves to escape God's wrath in the tribulations accompanying the approach of the Day of the Lord.

It is not clear whether John understood himself to be the returned Elijah—in John's Gospel (1:21) he denies that he is Elijah—but Jesus certainly understood John's ministry in this way. In Matthew 11:14, Jesus tells the multitudes, "For all the prophets and the law prophesied until John came; and if you are willing to accept it, he is Elijah who is to come." Then, in today's gospel, speaking with his disciples Peter, James, and John as they are descending the Mount of the Transfiguration, Jesus once again identifies John the Baptist with Elijah.

The point not to be overlooked in this dialogue is that Jesus and the three disciples have just been in the actual presence of Elijah. During the Transfiguration, as Jesus became radiant with brilliant light, Moses and Elijah appeared speaking with him, and Peter wanted to make three booths, one for Jesus, one for Moses, and one for Elijah (Matthew 17:2-4).

Coming down off the mountain, Jesus charges the three disciples to tell no one about the vision until the Son of Man is raised from the dead. The disciples ask: "Then why do the scribes say that first Elijah must come?" Since the Transfiguration has amply confirmed their conviction that Jesus is the Messiah, they are naturally wondering why Elijah did not return before Jesus came on the scene.

Jesus answers: "Elijah is indeed coming and will restore all things; but I tell you that Elijah has already come, and they did not recognize him, but they did to him whatever they pleased. So also the Son of Man is about to suffer at their hands." At this point the three disciples recognize that Jesus is speaking of John the Baptist, whose death has already taken place (recounted in Matthew 14:1-12).

"So also the Son of Man is about to suffer at their hands." Here is perhaps the most significant link between John the Baptist and Jesus. Both suffer violent death in the fulfillment of their mission. John the Baptist has fulfilled the role of Elijah as forerunner of the messiah, and Jesus is the messiah who inaugurates the kingdom of God—precisely in and through his suffering, death, and resurrection.

The Third Sunday of Advent

YEAR A	YEAR B	YEAR C
Isaiah 35:1-10	Isaiah 61:1-4, 8-11	Zephaniah 3:14-20
Psalm 146:4-9 or	Psalm 126 or	Canticle 9
Canticle 3 or 15	Canticle 3 or 15	Philippians 4:4-7
James 5:7-10	I Thessalonians	Luke 3:7-18
Matthew 11:2-11	5:16-24	
	John 1:6-8, 19-28	

The gospel readings on the Third Sunday of Advent—*Gaudete*, or "Rejoice" Sunday—continue to look at John the Baptist from various angles. In the reading from Matthew (Year A), John sends word to Jesus from prison, asking, "Are you the one who is to come, or are we to wait for another?" The reading from John's Gospel (Year B) relates the dialogue between John and priests and Levites sent from Jerusalem to question him concerning who he is. The reading from Luke (Year C) records John's ethical directives to those who ask him "What shall we do?" in response to his preaching of repentance.

The readings for the weekdays of the Third Week of Advent continue to explore the significance of John's ministry through various statements that Jesus makes about him later in the gospels.

On December 17 (or 18) the readings for the Third Week of Advent are discontinued, and the readings for the pre-Christmas octave, beginning on page 77, take their place. No readings are given for Saturday in the Third Week of Advent because it always falls on December 17 or later.

Monday in 3 Advent

By What Authority?
Numbers 24:2–7,15–17a
Psalm 25:3–8
Matthew 21:23–27

Today's readings touch on the question of authority. The gospel begins with the chief priests and elders confronting Jesus in the temple and demanding to know: "By what authority are you doing these things, and who gave you this authority?"

It is a reasonable question. After entering Jerusalem the previous day, Jesus cleansed the temple, driving out those who were buying and selling and overturning the tables of the moneychangers (Matthew 21:12). Subsequently, he healed the blind and lame who came to him in the temple precincts. The chief priests and scribes became angry when they heard the crowd crying out, "Hosanna to the Son of David" (Matthew 21:14-16). So now, they naturally want to understand his motives: specifically, at whose behest does he believe himself to be acting?

Many commentators regard the question as a trap. If Jesus answers that his authority comes from God, he can be charged with blasphemy. The matter may be more complex, however, for the question may instead represent the beginning of a sincere attempt to gather information and to evaluate Jesus' words and deeds.

The great sociologist Max Weber made an influential distinction between what he called institutional authority and charismatic authority. Both types of authority benefit society, but in different ways. A judge presiding in a courtroom embodies institutional authority; the leader of a popular reform movement (such as the Rev. Martin Luther King Jr.) exemplifies charismatic authority. The judge's institutional authority comes from his or her office, as defined in a state's constitution and laws; the charismatic leader's authority comes from the power of his or her personality, ideas, and persuasive ability.

The authority of the chief priests and elders was clearly of the institutional type. Their office was hereditary, and their duties were defined by a complex system of laws, procedures, and customs. They believed that so long as they performed these duties faithfully, particularly by offering the appointed round of prayers and sacrifices in the temple, God would continue to be present with and bless Israel.

Yet it is possible that they also recognized that God could act outside the official channels. In today's Old Testament reading, the God of Israel speaks through a pagan seer. The Moabite king Balak summons the seer Balaam to curse Israel, but Balaam finds that he can speak only the words that God gives him, blessing Israel instead.

So, confronted with a charismatic figure like Jesus of Nazareth—an itinerant teacher and healer from Galilee who has triumphantly entered Jerusalem, disrupted commercial exchange in the temple precincts, and received acclamation as the Son of David—the first question the religions authorities must ask is, "By what authority are you doing these things, and who gave you this authority?"

They need to know, first, whether he represents some other group or faction in the complex world of Judean power politics. Perhaps one of the influential rabbis commissioned him? But if he does claim that his authority comes directly from God, then they can begin asking a series of traditional questions to discern whether he really is the messiah or an imposter.

Rather than responding directly, however, he replies that he will answer only if they first answer a question that he puts to them. (Such use of a counter-question was a recognized tactic in rabbinical debates.) "Did the baptism of John come from heaven, or was it of human origin?"

In a subtle way, his counter-question implicitly answers their question. His authority is the same as John's authority. If they believe that God authorized John's baptism, they should have no trouble believing that God has authorized Jesus' ministry. If they don't believe that God authorized John's baptism, they are unlikely to believe that Jesus' authority comes from God. But because they will not commit themselves on the question of John's baptism, he is under no obligation to give their question an explicit answer.

Today's gospel emphasizes how closely Jesus links the meaning of his own ministry to that of the forerunner. The Baptist's words and actions cannot be adequately understood except in relation to Jesus who comes after him. Conversely, Jesus' identity and mission cannot be understood without reference to John's ministry of preparation. It is for this reason that the Church spends so much time during Advent meditating on the figure of John the Baptist.

Tuesday in 3 Advent

Tax Collectors and Prostitutes Are Entering the Kingdom

Zephaniah 3:1–2, 9–13
Psalm 34:1–8
Matthew 21:28–32

In yesterday's gospel reading, set in the precincts of the Jerusalem temple, Jesus challenged the chief priests and elders of the people to give their opinion of John the Baptist: was his baptism of heavenly or human origin? They refused to answer, rightly calculating that if they said "from heaven," he would ask why they did not believe him, and if they said "from human beings," they would incur the displeasure of the multitudes who believed John to be a prophet.

In today's gospel, Jesus goes on the offensive, taking the religious authorities to task for their failure to believe John. He tells the parable of two sons asked by their father to work in the vineyard. The first son refuses the request but then changes his mind and goes to work; the second son agrees to the request but then does not go. Which of the two, Jesus asks, does the will of his father?

When they correctly answer, "The first," he springs the trap. They are like the second son, full of high-minded speech and promises of obedience but ultimately failing to put their words into action. The tax collectors and prostitutes, by contrast, are like the first son—initially appearing to be sinners but then changing their minds and entering the kingdom of heaven ahead of the chief priests and elders.

The religious authorities stand condemned precisely for their response to John the Baptist. "For John came to you in the way of righteousness and you did not believe him, but the tax collectors and the prostitutes believed him; and even after you saw it, you did not change your minds and believe him." Significantly, Jesus is suggesting that people will not be judged by their response to him but by their response to John before him. The ministries of Jesus and John are so closely linked that people's responses to the forerunner are reliable indicators of their likely responses to the Messiah himself.

Tax collectors and prostitutes entering the kingdom ahead of the chief priests and elders is a classic biblical image of reversal. The Old Testament reading from

Zephaniah anticipates this image. Addressing Jerusalem, the prophet writes:

> *On that day you shall not be put to shame because of all
>   the deeds by which you have rebelled against me;*
> *for then I will remove from your midst your proudly
>   exultant ones,*
> *and you shall no longer be haughty in my holy
>   mountain.*
> *For I will leave in the midst of you a people humble and
>   lowly.* (Zephaniah 3:11-12a)

In the prophet's vision, the reversal takes place "on that day," that is, the Day of the Lord. But the point not to be missed in today's gospel is that Jesus speaks of the kingdom as a present reality. Already the tax collectors and prostitutes are entering the kingdom of heaven ahead of the chief priests and elders.

Eschatology is the branch of theology dealing with the "last things" (or, in more popular parlance, the "end times"). Theologians sometimes make a distinction between "future eschatology" and "realized eschatology." In future eschatology, the kingdom is not yet but will come at a specific point in the future. In realized eschatology, by contrast, the kingdom of God is an ever-present reality that people can enter at any time.

The dominant stream of New Testament theology combines aspects of both future and realized eschatology and is summed up in the saying that the kingdom is "already but not yet." That is, in the life and ministry of Jesus the kingdom has dawned so that it is possible to speak of people "already" entering it in the present. But its final consummation is "not yet," and must await the return of the risen and ascended Christ on the Last Day.

The Third Sunday of Advent is known as Gaudete ("Rejoice") Sunday. This third week of the season combines joy at the "already present" aspect of the kingdom (realized eschatology) with hope for the "not yet" aspect (future eschatology). The message of today's gospel is that even now we can enter the kingdom and begin to experience its reality—provided that we hear and respond to John's call to repentance.

Wednesday in 3 Advent

Let the Skies Rain Down Righteousness
Isaiah 45:5–8 (9–17) 18–25
Psalm 85:8–13
Luke 7:19–23

(Note: Today's gospel reading is Luke's parallel to Matthew 11:2-6, which was discussed in the homily for Thursday in the Second Week of Advent. The preacher may want to address that episode again today and develop it further. Another option, taken here, is to focus on the Old Testament reading from Isaiah.)

In many churches and cathedrals throughout the Anglican world a hymn known as "The Advent Prose," a translation of the medieval Latin hymn *Rorate Coeli*, is sung during this season. Its refrain quotes a verse from today's reading from Isaiah: "Drop down ye heavens from above, and let the skies pour down righteousness."

The full verse, Isaiah 45:8, reads in the New Revised Standard Version as follows:

Shower, O heavens from above, and let the skies rain
  down righteousness;
let the earth open, that salvation may spring up,
and let it cause righteousness to sprout up also;
  I the Lord have created it.

In the original Hebrew, these lines voice a prayer for deliverance (salvation) using the image of falling rain fructifying a parched landscape and causing lush vegetation to burst forth. In the fourth-century Latin Vulgate, however, Saint Jerome rendered "salvation" as "a savior"—giving the text the meaning expressed in the 1610 Douay-Rheims English translation: "let the earth be opened, and bud forth a saviour…"

Thus translated into Latin, these lines seemed to medieval commentators an allegorical prophecy of the Holy Spirit descending like rain upon the Virgin Mary, who as a human being is "earth," to bring forth the Savior, Jesus. Such a beautiful symbolic interpretation goes beyond but is not necessarily incompatible with the original meaning of the biblical text. The medieval Advent liturgies quote Isaiah 45:8 frequently: in the versicles and responses of the Divine Office, in the Introit (Entrance Song) for the Holy Eucharist on the Fourth Sunday of Advent and, as we have seen, in the hymn *Rorate Coeli*.

We must not overlook the verse's context in Chapter 45 of the Book of Isaiah, much of which is contained in today's Old Testament reading. Writing toward the end of the Babylonian captivity, the prophet known as Second Isaiah envisions Israel's God as the God of the whole earth. At earlier times in Old Testament history, the Israelites appear to have regarded their God as one among many. Other peoples had their own deities, who were just as real as (but usually less powerful than) the God of Israel. But here, speaking through the prophet, God repeatedly declares: "I am the Lord, and there is no other; besides me there is no god."

It follows that the God of Israel is also the God of all people, and is in charge of all human history: "I form light and create darkness, I make weal and create woe; I the Lord do all these things." It was God who delivered Israel into captivity by the Babylonians, and now it is same God who has appointed Cyrus the King of Persia to liberate them from exile: "I have aroused Cyrus in righteousness, and I will make all his paths straight; he shall build my city and set my exiles free…"

Israel has no basis for complaint about God's gracious dealings with other peoples: "Woe to you who strive with your Maker, earthen vessels with the potter! … Will you question me about my children, or command me concerning the work of my hands?" All God has been doing, first in the Babylonian captivity and now in the liberation and return from exile, serves a wider purpose, not just for Israel, but for all nations.

Yet Israel has a special role to play. As the nations of the earth realize the futility of their worship of idols, they will turn to Israel for knowledge of the one true God: "They will make supplication to you, saying, 'God is with you alone, and there is no other; there is no god besides him.'" Speaking through the prophet, God finally makes his appeal to all peoples everywhere:

> *Turn to me and be saved, all the ends of the earth!*
> *For I am God, and there is no other.*
> *By myself I have sworn, from my mouth has gone forth*
> *in righteousness a word that shall not return:*
> *"To me every knee shall bow, every tongue shall swear."*

The prayer in Isaiah 45:8 that righteousness may fall from like rain from heaven and bring forth salvation (or a savior) needs to be read in the context of these sweeping affirmations of God's providential care and concern for all peoples. The Hebrew scriptures proclaim the hope of a messiah, an anointed one, who will come as the savior not only of Israel but also of the whole world.

Thursday in 3 Advent

Acknowledging the Justice of God
Isaiah 54:1–10
Psalm 30
Luke 7:24–30

Today's gospel reading is Luke's parallel to Matthew 11:2-6, which we heard a week ago today. In both Matthew's and Luke's versions, Jesus acclaims John the Baptist as a prophet, and more than a prophet—the Lord's messenger sent ahead to prepare the way for the messiah. Among those born of women, Jesus continues, no one is greater than John, but even the least in the kingdom of God is greater than he.

At this point, however, Luke adds two verses missing from Matthew's version:

And all the people who heard this, including the tax collectors, acknowledged the justice of God, because they had been baptized with John's baptism. But by refusing to be baptized by him, the Pharisees and the lawyers rejected God's purpose for themselves.

My own somewhat more literal translation of Luke's Greek is as follows:

> *And having been baptized with John's baptism, all the people hearing and the tax collectors proclaimed God's justice, while not having been baptized by him, the Pharisees and the lawyers rejected God's purpose for themselves.*

What this translation attempts to show is that the people acclaim God's justice not because they have heard Jesus' words confirming the rightness of their decision to receive John's baptism. (That would be the "subjective" interpretation.) Instead, John's baptism has somehow enabled those who have received it to acclaim God's justice in response to Jesus' words in a way that remains impossible for the Pharisees and lawyers. (This is the "objective" interpretation.) Somehow, the baptism of John has served as objective preparation for receiving the messiah.

We might be tempted to conclude that the baptism of John was what the catholic tradition calls a "means of grace"—a rite objectively conferring spiritual gifts upon its recipients. Speaking for that tradition, however, Saint Thomas Aquinas denies that John's baptism was either a means of grace or a sacrament. It was a preparation for grace, but it did not confer grace.

How, then, could John's baptism have made the difference between those who "acknowledged the justice of God," and those who "rejected God's purpose for themselves"? My best guess is that the answer involves the nature of John's baptism as "a baptism of repentance for the forgiveness of sins" (Mark 1:4). Those who received John's baptism were willing to acknowledge their guilt and their need for God's forgiveness. Such humility, openness, and contrition would subsequently have disposed them to recognizing and receiving Jesus when they encountered him.

Conversely, those who refused John's baptism most likely did so because they believed themselves righteous and hence in no need of forgiveness. This attitude of pride and self-sufficiency would have blinded them to their need of a savior, even when the savior himself was on their very doorsteps. Hence, they rejected Jesus and, in so doing, as Luke says, they "rejected God's purpose for themselves."

This is another deep linkage between the ministries of John the Baptist and Jesus. John called the people to receive baptism, a washing with water, as a token of repentance of their sins. As expressed in John's baptism, this disposition of humility and repentance prepared the people to receive the one coming after John.

A basic principle of classical Christian theological method is that to recognize and understand God's truth, the theologian must be prepared not only intellectually (by years of study), but also spiritually (by regular prayer and participation in worship) and morally (by practice of the virtues and regular confession and repentance). In some Anglican liturgies predating the 1979 *Book of Common Prayer*, the Confession of Sin and Absolution were called the "ritual preparation of the people for Communion." Repentance is an essential component of preparation to meet the Lord in Word and Sacrament. It is no less an essential component of our Advent preparation to meet the infant Lord at Christmas.

Friday in 3 Advent

A Burning and a Shining Lamp
Isaiah 56:1–8
Psalm 67
John 5:33–36

(Note: Today's Old Testament reading is also appointed for Proper 15, Year A.)

Today's gospel concludes the series of reflections on John the Baptist that began a week ago (on Thursday in the second Week of Advent). Since then, the weekday readings have focused not so much on what John says about himself as on what Jesus says about John.

Jesus describes John the Baptist as a prophet and "more than a prophet"—the "messenger" of Malachi 3:1, sent ahead to prepare the way (Matthew 11:9-10; Luke 7:26-27). No one born of woman is greater than John, yet the least in the kingdom of heaven is greater than he (Matthew 11:11; Luke 7:28). As foretold in Malachi 4:5, John is "Elijah who is to come" (Matthew 11:14)—an identification that Jesus later reiterates to Peter, James, and John coming down the Mount of the Transfiguration as he predicts that the

Son of Man will suffer just as John has suffered (Matthew 17:11-13).

Comparing his ministry with that of John, Jesus observes, "For John came neither eating nor drinking, and they say, 'He has a demon'; the Son of Man came eating and drinking, and they say, 'Look, a glutton and a drunkard, a friend of tax collectors and sinners!'" (Matthew 11:18-19). Later, in the temple, Jesus challenges the chief priests and elders to say whether John's baptism was of human or divine origin (Matthew 21:25). When they refuse to answer, he declares that the tax collectors and prostitutes are entering the kingdom of heaven ahead of them: "for John came to you in the way of righteousness and you did not believe him, but the tax collectors and the prostitutes believed him; and even after you saw it, you did not change your minds and believe him" (Matthew 21:32).

The cumulative picture that emerges suggests that the ministries of John and Jesus are interdependent and mutually interpretive. The full significance of John's mission as the forerunner becomes clear only retrospectively in light of Jesus' arrival as the messiah. Conversely, John's preaching and baptism of repentance for the forgiveness of sins prepares the people to receive Jesus as the messiah. Luke 7:29-30 implies that those who received John's baptism were more likely to respond positively to Jesus than those who had rejected it.

Today's reading from the Gospel of John rounds this picture out by speaking of John the Baptist as a witness. In this part of John's Gospel, Jesus has just healed an invalid by the pool of Bethsaida in Jerusalem. The "Jews"—John's shorthand for the Jewish religious authorities—have challenged Jesus for performing such a deed on the sabbath, and Jesus has declared that just as his Father works on the sabbath, so he must work. The religious authorities then attack him not only for breaking the sabbath but also for calling God his Father, thus making himself equal with God (John 5:1-18).

In the discourse that follows, Jesus defends himself by calling forth witnesses to testify on his behalf. He immediately admits that if he can do no more than testify on his own behalf, his testimony is not reliable (John 5:31). But there is "another" who testifies: "You sent messengers to John, and he testified to the truth."

John was "a burning and shining lamp, and you were willing to rejoice for a while in his light." But now, Jesus declares: "I have a testimony greater than John's." Those who encounter Jesus are now called to believe on the basis of this even more powerful testimony: "The works that the Father has given me to complete, the very works that I am doing, testify on my behalf that the Father has sent me."

So, the witnesses who testify on behalf of Jesus' claim to be the Son of God are, first, John the Baptist and, second, the works which Jesus himself performs. (A third witness, mentioned in the verses immediately following today's gospel, is scripture, in which God the Father also testifies to Jesus.)

During this season of Advent so far, we have rejoiced for a while in the light of John's "burning and shining lamp." He has witnessed to Jesus' identity and mission as the Son of God. But now it is time to move beyond John to encounter Jesus directly. In the remaining week of Advent, the daily eucharistic readings tell the story of God's immediate preparation to send the savior into the world.

The Fourth Sunday of Advent

YEAR A	YEAR B	YEAR C
Isaiah 7:10-16	2 Samuel 7: 1-11, 16	Micah 5:2-5a
Psalm 80:1-7, 16-18	Canticle 3 or 15 or Psalm 89: 1-4, 19-26	Canticle 3 or 15 or Psalm 80:1-7
Romans 1:1-7	Romans 16:25-27	Hebrews 10:5-10
Matthew 1:18-25	Luke 1:26-38	Luke 1:39-45 (46-55)

As Christmas approaches, the readings for the Fourth Sunday of Advent focus on the coming birth of the Christ child. In year A, the gospel recounts the story of the angelic annunciation to Joseph. In years B and C, the gospels are taken from Luke, presenting the episodes known as the Annunciation to Mary and the Visitation of Mary to Elizabeth, respectively.

The Old Testament readings for the Fourth Sunday of Advent in all three years are closely tied to the gospel themes. In Year A, the prophet Isaiah foretells the birth of a child to be known as Emmanuel, "God with us." In Year B, the prophet Nathan relays God's promise to David that his throne and lineage shall be established forever. And in Year C, the prophet Micah prophesies to Bethlehem that from the town shall come one who is to be ruler in Israel, "whose origin is from of old, from ancient days."

Developing this focus, the readings for the weekdays of the pre-Christmas Octave—December 17 through 24—systematically guide daily worshipers through the birth narratives in the first chapters of Matthew and Luke, focusing on both Jesus and John the Baptist.

The Advent weekday readings in the following pages always begin on December 17 and take precedence over those appointed for the Third Week of Advent. The weekdays from December 17 through 24 can profitably be regarded as a "Novena" celebrated in preparation for Christmas.

One of the days between December 17 and December 24 will always fall on Sunday. When this happens, the readings appointed for the Fourth Sunday in Advent (Year A, B, or C as appropriate) are used in place of those appointed for the weekday. The gospel on Saturday or Monday may be extended to include the missed gospel reading (provided the two gospel readings are continuous).

December 21 presents a rubrical conundrum for clergy in The Episcopal Church because in the Calendar of

The Book of Common Prayer, 1979, it is the feast of Saint Thomas the Apostle, which always takes precedence over the Weekdays of Advent. (Churches such as the Roman Catholic Church and the Anglican Church of Canada observe the Feast of Saint Thomas on July 3 and avoid this problem.) So far as I can see, the only solution is to celebrate two masses on December 21, one for Saint Thomas and one using the weekday proper for December 21. Otherwise, since the gospel readings from December 19 through 24 are taken in continuous sequence from Luke 1, it should be possible to combine gospel readings to include that for December 21 on either December 20 or December 22.

When December 21 falls on a Sunday, then the readings for the Fourth Sunday of Advent (Year A, B, or C) are used instead, and the Feast of Saint Thomas is transferred to Monday, December 22. In this case, again, it should be possible to combine the gospel readings on the remaining weekdays before Christmas to include those missed on Sunday and Monday.

December 17

Son of David, Son of Abraham
(*O Sapientia*)
Genesis 49:2, 8–10
Psalm 72:1–8
Matthew 1:1–7, 17

We probably don't place as much importance in genealogy today as people did in the ancient world. For many of us, genealogy is at best a sort of hobby, the quest to find one's roots. In certain parts of the country, of course, some people set great store by what family they come from—especially if it's an old established family that has been in the area for many generations.

Overall though, many Americans seem to take the attitude expressed by Ian Anderson of Jethro Tull in the lyrics of the 1971 album, *Aqualung*:

> *How do you dare tell me that I'm my father's son,*
> *When that was just an accident of birth?*
> *I'd rather look around me, compose a better song*
> *Cos that's the honest measure of my worth.*

In the ancient world, however, genealogy was enormously important. Its goal was not so much to gather historical information about the past as to establish one's identity in the present. The purpose of the genealogies in the gospels of Matthew and Luke is as much to show who Jesus is as to show who his ancestors were.

Matthew's genealogy demonstrates that Jesus is, first of all, the Son of David, a necessary qualification for being the messiah and, second, that he is a descendant of Abraham, Isaac, and Jacob, and hence a member of God's chosen people. Luke traces Jesus' descent all the way back to Adam, stressing his solidarity with the entire human race. But Matthew's emphasis is on how Jesus stands in continuity with the history of Israel.

One key detail in the genealogy is that Jesus' descent is through Judah, one of Jacob's twelve sons, the progenitors of the twelve tribes of Israel. In today's Old Testament reading from Genesis, Jacob (also known as Israel) blesses Judah:

> *The scepter shall not depart from Judah,*
> *nor the ruler's staff from between his feet,*
> *until tribute comes to him;*
> *and the obedience of the peoples is his.*

Jewish tradition reads these verses as a prophecy that the kings of Israel, including the coming messiah, were to be descended from the tribe of Judah, just as the genealogy establishes Jesus to be.

The larger point is that Jesus is not an interloper, alien to Israel's identity and traditions, but rather the one through whom is fulfilled all that God has been doing in Israel's sacred history all along. The threefold division of his ancestry into fourteen generations shows that the timing of Jesus' birth was not accidental—he came into the world at the opportune time, as the culmination and fulfillment of all that had taken place in Israel's history up to that point.

Some commentators note that Matthew's genealogy departs from the standards of the time by mentioning five women: including Tamar, Rahab the Harlot, and Ruth the Moabitess. Their inclusion introduces a factor of irregularity into the genealogy, which one commentator speculates is Matthew's way of preparing his readers for the irregular birth of Jesus—physically born of Mary yet receiving his Davidic descent from Joseph who is not his biological father.

The eucharistic readings from today until Christmas are taken from the infancy narratives of Matthew and Luke, and recount the events surrounding the births of both Jesus and John the Baptist. Matthew's genealogy shows us who, humanly speaking, Jesus is: son of Joseph, son of David, son of Judah, son of Abraham. The readings in the subsequent days will fill out that picture by showing that he is the Son of God as well.

December 18

He Will Save His People from Their Sins
(*O Adonai*)

Jeremiah 23:5–8
Psalm 72:11–18
Matthew 1:18–25

(Note: today's gospel is also read on the Fourth Sunday of Advent, Year A.)

We saw in yesterday's gospel that the genealogy with which Saint Matthew begins his gospel serves the purpose of establishing Jesus' identity as a son of Abraham and of David. In today's gospel, recounting the annunciation to Joseph, Matthew continues by showing how Jesus is also the Son of God.

Luke tells the story from Mary's viewpoint; Matthew tells it from Joseph's. When Mary is found to be pregnant, Joseph contemplates quietly divorcing her, but an angel of the Lord appears to him in a dream and tells him not to be afraid to take her as his wife, because the child has been conceived of the Holy Spirit. The angel further tells him that he is to name the child Jesus, for he will save his people from their sins.

Yesterday, we saw that the purpose of a genealogy in the ancient world was not only to give interesting information about a person's past lineage but also to reveal something of that person's present identity, role, and mission. To show that Jesus is a son of Abraham and of David is to reveal much about who he is.

The same is even truer of a person's name. The etymological meaning of the name Jesus—in Aramaic *Yeshua*, and in Hebrew *Joshua*—is something like "God is salvation," or "God saves." The name thus discloses Jesus' role in God's plan as the savior, the one who saves his people from their sins.

Matthew's birth narrative also follows up on the genealogy in an unexpected way. The concluding verse of the passage says that once the child was born, Joseph "named him Jesus." This naming would have taken place at the circumcision, eight days after the birth.

By formally naming the child at this ceremony, Joseph acknowledges him as his son, claims paternity, and in effect adopts him into his lineage and heritage. In this way, Jesus receives from Joseph his human status as the Son of David. The naming reveals the fullness of Jesus' identity in his human and divine natures. He is already the eternally begotten Son of God; from Joseph he receives the Davidic descent that qualifies him to be the messiah of Israel.

December 19

To Make Ready a People Prepared for the Lord
(*O Radix Jesse*)

Judges 13:2–7, 24–25
Psalm 71:1–8
Luke 1:5–25

In biblical times, barrenness—that is, infertility—was commonly seen as a curse or punishment from God. Couples unable to conceive suffered under a social stigma. At the beginning of today's gospel, Luke is careful to tell us that Zechariah and Elizabeth were both "righteous before God, living blamelessly according to all the commandments and regulations of the Lord." That point has to be made clear first, before Luke tells us that they had no children. Otherwise, readers in Luke's day would assume that their barrenness was due to some fault or sin on their part.

Contrary to all expectations, on multiple occasions in scripture God chooses a barren couple—often in old age—to conceive and bear a child who will be the agent of God's purposes in history. The more miraculous the circumstances of the conception and birth, the more important the child is destined to become in adulthood.

Both today's Old Testament reading from Judges and today's gospel from Luke follow the biblical pattern of a birth-annunciation narrative. An angel appears and announces that the hitherto barren couple will conceive and bear a son. In Judges, the recipient is the nameless wife of Manoah and the child to be born is Samson. In Luke, it is the priest Zechariah and the child to be born is John the Baptist.

In both cases, an instruction is given about avoiding wine and strong drink. Manoah and his wife are to avoid wine and strong drink, and no razor must ever be used to cut the child's hair, for from his birth he will be a nazirite, one dedicated completely to God. With Elizabeth and Zechariah, however, it is the child who must never drink wine or strong drink, for he will be filled with the Holy Spirit.

The mission of the future Samson will be to begin the deliverance of Israel from the Philistines. And the angel appearing to Zechariah describes John's future mission in language drawn from the fifth chapter of the Book of Malachi:

> *He will turn many of the people of Israel to the Lord their God. With the spirit and power of Elijah he will go before him, to turn the hearts of parents to their children, and the disobedient to the wisdom of the righteous, to make ready a people prepared for the Lord.*

The two annunciation narratives diverge in the responses of the recipients. Manoah's wife believes the angelic announcement and goes right away to report it to her husband. But Zechariah questions the angel in disbelief: "How will I know that this is so? For I am an old man, and my wife is getting on in years." The angel announces that he is Gabriel, who stands in the presence of God and who has been sent to bring this good news to Zechariah. For his incredulity Zechariah will be struck dumb until the day when these things occur.

Both annunciation narratives conclude with the fulfillment of the angelic promise. Manoah's wife conceives and gives birth to a son, whom she names Samson. Elizabeth conceives and remains in seclusion for five months, during which she rejoices quietly that God has looked favorably upon her and taken away the disgrace she has endured among her people.

In these birth-annunciation narratives, the initial barrenness of the couple highlights the character of the conception and birth as a miraculous gift from God. This gift removes the social stigma of barrenness and brings many blessings, but it is never given for the couple's sake alone. The child to be born is dedicated to the Lord's service; indeed, both Samson and John the Baptist ultimately die violent deaths in fulfillment of their respective vocations.

One lesson for us is that while God often blesses us with miraculous and wonderful gifts, they are never given for us alone, to be used purely for our own enjoyment or in fulfillment of our own purposes. We are called to offer these gifts back to God in service, even if this means taking them in directions we would never have chosen. Having freely received, we freely give.

December 20

His Name Shall Be Called Emmanuel
(*O Clavis David*)

Isaiah 7:10–14
Psalm 24
Luke 1:26–38

(Note: Today's Old Testament reading is read on the Fourth Sunday of Advent, Year A. Today's gospel is also read on the Fourth Sunday of Advent, Year B.)

Today's readings describe a prophecy and its fulfillment, centered in the words, "Look, the young woman is with child and shall bear a son, and shall name him Immanuel." In the first reading, Isaiah delivers the prophecy to Ahaz, the King of Judah. And in the gospel reading, the angel Gabriel announces this prophecy's ultimate fulfillment in the virginal conception and birth of Jesus. The parallel passage in Matthew's Gospel makes the connection explicit: "All this took place to fulfill what had been spoken by the Lord through the prophet: 'Look, the virgin shall conceive and bear a son, and they shall name him Emmanuel'" (Matthew 1:22-23).

A striking but not immediately obvious contrast involves the recipients of the divine message. Ahaz is one of the wickedest kings of Judah, a worshiper of foreign gods who installs a blasphemous altar in the temple and who practices child sacrifice. By contrast, Mary is completely pure, holy, and obedient to God. Yet God speaks to them both: to Ahaz through the prophet Isaiah, to Mary through the angel Gabriel.

The prophecy to Ahaz has an immediate meaning in the context of the political and military situation of the day. The kingdom of Judah is under attack by the kings of Damascus and Samaria. In response, God promises Ahaz that a child is about to be born, and that while the child is still an infant the two kings will be defeated. This birth is thus a sign of God's presence with God's people; the child will be called Emmanuel, or "God is with us." Scholars debate the identity of the child. It may be Hezekiah, the son of Ahaz, who eventually succeeds him on the throne of Judah. But we cannot be certain.

A certain school of biblical interpretation speaks of dual or multiple fulfillments of prophecy: an immediate fulfillment in the time of the prophecy itself, and an even greater fulfillment (or fulfillments) in the distant future. Here, the immediate fulfillment takes place during the reign of Ahaz himself. Yet about seven centuries later the prophecy finds an even greater fulfillment, indeed its ultimate fulfillment, in the birth of Jesus. By this time, the Hebrew "a young woman shall conceive and bear a son" has been translated into Greek using the word *parthenos*, "virgin." Thus, in its Greek form it points all the more directly to the Virgin Mary as the bearer of the one who is definitively Emmanuel, "God with us."

Note again the contrast between Ahaz and Mary. When the prophet tells Ahaz to ask for a sign, anything he wants, the king effectively tells him to go away, he doesn't want to hear it. The prophet says, fine, if you won't ask for a sign, God will give you one of his own choosing—the young woman shall conceive and bear a son. Where Ahaz is closed and resistant to any word from God, Mary is completely open and receptive. True, she is frightened at the angel's appearance—because angels are terrifying—and she asks for clarification of how it is possible for her to conceive since she is a virgin. Nonetheless, her attitude throughout is summed up in her concluding words: "Here am I, the servant of the Lord, let it be with me according to your word."

When the word of God comes to us, calling us to undertake new forms of service and promising to be present with us, Ahaz and Mary exemplify two opposite responses: a closed heart versus an open heart; resistance versus receptivity; defiance versus obedience. We would do well to follow the way of Mary.

December 21

Blessed Are You among Women
(*O Oriens*)

Zephaniah 3:14–18a
(or in Year C, Song of Solomon 2:8–14)
Psalm 33:1–5,20–22
Luke 1:39–45

*(Note: Zephaniah 3:14-20 and today's gospel are
read on the Fourth Sunday of Advent, Year C.)*

One type of icon of Mary in the Eastern Orthodox tradition is known as the Virgin of the Sign. Her arms are extended in the *orans* position. A circular medallion superimposed on her torso shows the Christ Child within, his hands similarly extended in blessing. This image of Mary expresses the theme of today's gospel perfectly. Here Mary appears as the *Theotokos*, the God-bearer: she who carries Christ in her womb for nine months before giving him birth.

Mary's first recorded act in scripture after the Annunciation is to visit her cousin Elizabeth in the hill-country of Judea. To confirm the truth of his message, the angel Gabriel gave Mary a sign: "your relative Elizabeth in her old age has also conceived a son; and this is the sixth month for her who was said to be barren. For nothing will be impossible with God" (Luke 1:36-37). Mary had no independent way of knowing this, because "for five months [Elizabeth] remained in seclusion" (Luke 1:24). Elizabeth's unborn son is the future John the Baptist.

Traveling from Nazareth to Judea, Mary bears Jesus to Elizabeth and John. She thus begins to fulfill her vocation of bringing Christ to those who are waiting for him. She becomes a source of blessing to those whom she visits. Elizabeth is filled with the Holy Spirit and exclaims, "And why has this happened to me, that the mother of my Lord comes to me?" And the unborn John the Baptist leaps for joy in Elizabeth's womb at the arrival of the one for whom he has been sent to prepare the way.

Having been blessed by the arrival of Mary bearing the Christ in her womb, Elizabeth pronounces two blessings of her own. First, as Elizabeth is supernaturally given the insight to discern, Mary is the mother of her Lord: "Blessed are you among women, and blessed is the fruit of your womb."

But then Elizabeth adds a second blessing: "Blessed is she who believed that there would be a fulfillment of what was spoken to her from the Lord." In a sermon on the

Visitation, Roger Greenacre, an Anglican priest, suggests that here Elizabeth is perhaps making a half ironic reference to her husband Zechariah, who was struck dumb for not believing what was spoken to him from the Lord!

In a later episode in the gospels, a woman in the crowd acclaims Jesus with a blessing on his mother:

> *A woman in the crowd raised her voice and said to him, "Blessed is the womb that bore you and the breasts that nursed you!" But he said, "Blessed rather are those who hear the word of God and obey it!"* (Luke 11:27-28)

Contrary to first appearances, Jesus is not repudiating but rather is completing the woman's blessing on his mother. Mary is indeed blessed for bearing him in her womb and nursing him as an infant. But, as Elizabeth has just affirmed, she is blessed above all for having heard and obeyed the word of God.

In the same sermon, Greenacre makes a related point. Mary models mutual visitation as the pattern of the Christian life. Instead of withdrawing into solitude for the duration of her pregnancy, Mary travels from Galilee to Judea, simply to share in Elizabeth's joy and to share her joy with Elizabeth. Blessings are exchanged and begin to multiply. So it is with us. The blessings we receive from God are not to be held in isolation but shared, as we visit one another just as Mary visited Elizabeth.

It follows from these reflections that the Visitation of Mary to Elizabeth is not an incidental episode in the Lucan infancy narrative, but an archetypal moment, a revelation of the Virgin Mary in her God-given vocation of bringing Christ into the world. Just as she brought Christ to Elizabeth and John, so she brings Christ to us. As the God-bearer, she is for us a source both of blessing and of the grace we need to fulfill our vocations to prepare the way of the Lord.

December 22

The Almighty Has Done Great Things for Me
(O Rex Gentium)

1 Samuel 1:19–28
Canticle 9 or Psalm 113 or 122
Luke 1:46–56

(Note: today's gospel is also an optional extension of the gospel for the Fourth Sunday of Advent, Year C.)

Our readings for today link two parallel episodes in the scriptures: the conception and birth of the judge Samuel in the Old Testament and the conception and birth of our Lord Jesus Christ in the New Testament.

In the Old Testament story, the man Elkanah has two wives, Penninah and Hannah. Penninah has borne children, but Hannah has not. This leads to tension in the three-way relationship as Penninah taunts Hannah for her barrenness, causing her distress. On their annual visit to the sanctuary at Shiloh, however, Hannah prays for a son and vows that if her request is granted, she will dedicate him to the Lord's service all the days of his life.

And so, as we heard in today's reading, after they return home, Elkanah has sexual relations with Hannah, the Lord remembers her prayer, and she conceives and bears a son, whom she names Samuel. After the child is weaned, she takes him to Shiloh and dedicates him to the Lord's service, leaving him there to be brought up by Eli the priest.

It's always seemed to me a bit odd: If Hannah wanted a son so much, then why was she willing to bear him, wean him, and then effectively give him up for adoption? Part of the answer may be that what Hannah wanted was not so much a son to bring up as the removal of the stigma and shame of barrenness. Immediately following the passage in today's reading, she breaks forth into a song, which provides the Old Testament model for Mary's *Magnificat* in today's gospel. Hannah praises the God who reverses the fortunes of the rich and poor, who humbles the powerful and exalts the lowly—just as God has done with her.

At another level, however, Hannah understands that since all good gifts come from God, by dedicating the boy to the Lord's service she is merely offering back what she has freely received. In this sense, her offering represents a genuine sacrifice. It may well be painful, but Hannah knows that God gives us good gifts not to hoard and keep to ourselves, but to pass on and share.

Hannah accompanies her dedication of the boy to the Lord's service with sacrifice and a song of praise. Similarly, in today's gospel, Mary sings her song of praise to God. She's just arrived at the house of her cousin Elizabeth who, despite her seniority in age and superior social status, has honored Mary as the mother of her Lord—another instance of God reversing people's earthly positions. Yet Mary's response is not to focus on herself, basking in Elizabeth's acclaim but rather to break forth into worship and praise of God who has so richly blessed her.

As Christmas approaches, we remember that God has given us many good gifts culminating in the greatest gift of all, his Son Jesus Christ. In today's readings, both Hannah and Mary model the fitting response to such a great gift: thanksgiving, worship, praise, sacrifice, and above all, the sacrificial offering back to God of all that God has given us.

December 23

You Shall Call His Name John
(*O Emmanuel*)

Malachi 3:1–5
Psalm 25:1–14
Luke 1:57–66

(*Note: Today's Old Testament reading is part of that read on the Second Sunday of Advent, Year C.*)

A striking feature of the birth narratives in Luke's Gospel—those of John the Baptist and of Jesus himself—is that in both cases the angel not only announces the forthcoming birth but also gives the name by which the child is to be called.

In biblical times, one's name was much more closely bound with the essence of one's identity than is the case today. Names were not just ways of distinguishing one person from another—forms of address to which a person answered—they actually disclosed something of a person's character, role, mission, and purpose in life. Thus, as we shall be reminded on the Feast of the Holy

Name on January 1, the name Jesus means something like "God saves," or "God is salvation," and is the name given to the son of Mary because "he will save their people from their sins."

Similarly, when the angel announces the birth of a son to Zechariah and Elizabeth, he instructs Zechariah, "You will name him John" (Luke 1:13). As we hear in today's gospel, when Elizabeth attempts to name her son John, those present at the circumcision ceremony object: none of your family is called by this name. The dumbstruck Zechariah has to confirm the name John by writing it down. Although rendered mute as punishment for his disbelief at the angel's message, his obedience to the angel's command to name his son John suffices to end the punishment, so that his tongue is loosed and he proceeds to praise God.

Fear comes over all their neighbors, and these events become the subject of talk throughout the hill country of Judea, with people asking, "What then will this child become?" Today's Old Testament reading has already supplied a preliminary answer: he will be the one of whom Malachi prophesied, "See, I am sending my messenger to prepare the way before me…"

The name John is in Hebrew *Yohanan*, which means something like "God is gracious," or "God has acted favorably." The name thus discloses the nature or purpose of John's mission as the forerunner sent to prepare the way of the Lord. Through John's preaching of a baptism of repentance for the forgiveness of sins in preparation for the coming savior, God is graciously showing grace and favor to the people. And in these last few days of Advent we rejoice that God has similarly favored and blessed us in so many different ways.

December 24

To Guide Our Feet into the Way of Peace
2 Samuel 7:1–16
Psalm 89:1–4,19–29
Luke 1:67–79

(Note: Part of today's Old Testament reading is also read on the Fourth Sunday of Advent, Year B.)

Today's gospel consists of the canticle *Benedictus Dominus Deus*, traditionally sung every day in the Western monastic tradition at the Office of Lauds. By extension, in some parts of The Episcopal Church it is customarily sung or said daily as the second canticle at Morning Prayer.

The canticle's imagery of day dawning makes it especially appropriate for morning prayers. We might imagine singing it in a monastic chapel as the first streaks of sunlight begin to illuminate the sky through the east windows.

In the gospel infancy narratives, this canticle comprises the first words spoken by the priest Zechariah after his tongue has been loosed after naming his son, the future

John the Baptist. Zechariah was struck dumb for his skepticism when the angel Gabriel appeared to him in the temple to tell him that he and his wife Elizabeth would conceive in their old age.

Down through the centuries, commentators have interpreted certain details of the story allegorically. The barrenness of Zechariah and Elizabeth, they suggest, symbolizes a world that has grown old in the barrenness of sin. The muteness of Zechariah similarly symbolizes the silencing of Old Testament prophecy. Many Jews of the time believed that the spirit of prophecy had departed from Israel several centuries before.

More than that however, the time of Zechariah's silence represents a liminal period. He has been in the presence of the Holy. No words can yet express what he has seen and heard. But the silence affords him a space in which he can prepare to interpret the meaning of what has happened.

Zechariah's song of praise is divided into two parts. The first half proclaims the coming of the savior, raised up by God from among the descendants of his servant David. The imminent arrival of this savior fulfills God's ancient promises to Abraham, "that we, being rescued from the hands of our enemies, might serve him without fear, in holiness and righteousness before him all our days."

As the Old Testament reading from the Second Book of Samuel makes clear, this arrival of the savior also fulfills the Lord's promise to David: "Your house and your kingdom shall be made sure forever before me; your throne shall be established forever."

The second part of the canticle, beginning with the words, "And you, child, will be called the prophet of the Most High," is addressed directly by Zechariah to the infant John, who "will go before the Lord to prepare his ways, to give knowledge of salvation to his people by the forgiveness of their sins."

Zechariah concludes by speaking of the dawning of the light of a new day upon Israel. His words evoke a prophecy of Isaiah: "The people who walked in darkness have seen a great light; those who lived in a land of deep darkness—on them light has shined" (Isaiah 9:2).

As Zechariah puts it: "By the tender mercy of our God, the dawn from on high will break upon us, to give light to those who sit in darkness and in the shadow of death, and to guide our feet into the way of peace."

These concluding verses make this canticle an especially fitting conclusion to our observance of the Advent season on the day before Christmas—when we watch for the dawning of a new day illumined by the arrival of the Savior.

Christmas Eve & Day

December 24 & 25

(Holy Eucharist during the night)	**(Holy Eucharist at dawn)**	**(Holy Eucharist during the day)**
Isaiah 9:2-7	Isaiah 62:6-12	Isaiah 52:7-10
Psalm 96	Psalm 97	Psalm 98
Titus 2:11-14	Titus 3:4-7	Hebrews 1:1-4, (5-12)
Luke 2:1-14 (15-20)	Luke 2: (1-7) 8-20	John 1:1-14

Following ancient practice, the Sunday lectionary gives three sets of readings for Christmas, traditionally assigned respectively to the night of Christmas Eve (*in nocte*), the dawn of Christmas Day (*in aurora*), and later on Christmas Morning (*in dies*). While it may not be practically feasible in many congregations to schedule three separate masses at times close to these traditional hours, doing so remains the ideal.

The gospel readings for Proper I and Proper II are taken from Luke's nativity narrative, which relates the events surrounding the birth of Jesus from the viewpoint of the shepherds in the fields near Bethlehem. The gospel reading for Proper III is taken from the prologue to John's Gospel and focuses on the theological meaning of the Incarnation.

Saint Stephen, Deacon and Martyr

December 26

Jeremiah 26:1-9, 12-15
Psalm 31 or 31:1-5
Acts 6:8-7:2a, 51c-60
Matthew 23:34-39

On the day after Christmas, the commemoration of the first Christian martyr confronts the Church with the contrast between light and darkness, life and death. To follow in the way of the Christ Child is to take up the cross. The persecution of Jeremiah in the Old Testament prefigures Stephen's arrest, trial, and martyrdom in the reading from Acts. In the gospel reading from Matthew, Jesus laments over Jerusalem, "the city that kills the prophets and stones those who are sent to it!"

Saint John, Apostle and Evangelist

December 27

Exodus 33:18-23
Psalm 92 or 92:1-4, 11-14
1 John 1:1-9
John 21:9b-24

This feast commemorates "the Beloved Disciple," traditionally identified as John, the son of Zebedee, and the author of the fourth gospel. It is fitting to commemorate John so soon after Christmas Day because of the prominence the Church has given to the prologue to John's Gospel (1:1-18) as a definitive statement of the meaning of Christ's Incarnation.

The Holy Innocents

December 28

Jeremiah 31:15-17
Psalm 124
Revelation 21:1-7
Matthew 2:13-18

King Herod's massacre of the male children in the region of Bethlehem reminds us that the nativity of Christ as recounted in the gospels is not simply a nice story but rather one that engages the human condition in all its grim reality. The coming of Christ into the world immediately provokes murderous opposition on the part of those who resist God's reign by clinging to their own power. On this day, the Church recalls its solidarity with all who suffer as victims of unjust persecution.

The First Sunday after Christmas

Isaiah 61:10-62:3
Psalm 147 or 147:13-21
Galatians 3:23-25, 4:4-7
John 1:1-18

Today's readings function similarly to those given in Proper III for Christmas Day, supplying further theological reflection on the nativity. Isaiah sounds a note of celebration and joy. The reading from Galatians gives Paul's distinctive interpretation of the coming of Christ: "when the fullness of time had come, God sent his Son, born of a woman, born under the law, in order to redeem those who were under the law, so that we might receive adoption as children." And the gospel reading from the prologue to John proclaims the mystery of the Incarnation: "And the Word became flesh and lived among us, and we have seen his glory, the glory as of a father's only son, full of grace and truth."

The First Sunday after Christmas is celebrated only in those years when Christmas falls on a weekday. When

Christmas falls on a Sunday, the Feast of the Holy Name is celebrated on the following Sunday instead. In the years when it is celebrated, the First Sunday after Christmas always falls between December 26 and 31.

When one of the three major feasts following Christmas Day falls on a Sunday, the readings for the First Sunday after Christmas are used instead, and the feast is transferred to Monday. This means that Holy Innocents will be transferred to December 29, replacing its appointed Christmas weekday readings.

In congregations with a strong devotion to Saint Thomas of Canterbury, the readings for his feast day may be used in place of those appointed for December 29. Alternatively, the readings for December 29 may be used, combined with a commemoration of Saint Thomas in the Daily Office or in the concluding collect at the Prayers of the People.

December 29

Redemption of the Firstborn
1 John 2:7-11
Psalm 96:1-6
Luke 2:22-35

Today's readings anticipate the Feast of the Presentation of Our Lord in the Temple (also known as the Purification of the Blessed Virgin Mary, or Candlemas) on February 2. Luke describes two separate ceremonies that would have taken place a month or so after the birth of Jesus: the purification of a woman after childbirth and the redemption of a firstborn son. To some extent, he conflates the two. Yet it's entirely plausible that Mary and Joseph took the infant Jesus up to the temple in Jerusalem to perform these two ceremonies at the same time.

The Book of Leviticus gives the directions for the purification of a woman after childbirth. The traditional language of purity and impurity, cleanness and uncleanness, doesn't translate well into contemporary English and can be a bit misleading and unhelpful. A better way of putting it is that childbirth has put the woman into a state of ritualized separation from the mundane affairs of everyday life—including perhaps a welcome time of seclusion and rest—and the rite of purification marks her return and reintegration into the life of the community.

In any case, forty days after giving birth, a woman brought to the priest a lamb and a turtledove or young pigeon to be sacrificed, or, if she could not afford a lamb, a pair of turtledoves or two young pigeons. The offering of these sacrifices completed her purification after childbirth. (This practice ceased in Judaism after the destruction of the temple in 70 CE.)

The redemption of a firstborn son is a completely different ceremony, known in Hebrew as the *Pidyon Ha Ben*, and still practiced today in certain Jewish communities. In the Book of Exodus, the firstborn sons of all Israelites were originally designated to serve as priests to the Lord. But in the wilderness, the Hebrews rebelled and fashioned a golden calf to worship in God's place. To punish this sin of idolatry, God took the priesthood away from the firstborns and gave it instead to the tribe of Levi, and more specifically to the *Kohanim*, the descendants of Aaron the High Priest.

Nonetheless, the firstborns still belong to God. In Exodus, Chapter 13, the Lord commands Moses, "Consecrate to me all the firstborn; whatever is the first to open the womb among the Israelites, both of human beings and animals, is mine" (Exodus 13:2). The firstborn of animals are to be sacrificed to the Lord. But instead of sacrificing firstborn sons, the Lord instructs: "Every firstborn male among your children you shall redeem" (Exodus 13:13). The Book of Numbers further specifies the redemption price as five shekels of silver.

In the traditional ceremony, the father brings the child to the *Kohen*—in biblical times a priest of the temple; today a descendant of the priestly tribe of Aaron—and recites a formula indicating that the child is the firstborn of an Israelite mother and that he has come to redeem him as commanded in the Torah. The father then hands five silver coins to the Kohen, who holds them over the child and declares the redemption price has been accepted in the child's place. The Kohen then blesses the child and returns him to his father. In biblical times the ceremony took place at the temple in Jerusalem; today it usually takes place in a private home in the setting of a festive meal.

In the case of Jesus, all the conditions requiring the Pidyon Ha Ben were present. Jesus was the firstborn of an Israelite mother; he was a descendant of the royal tribe of Judah, not the priestly tribe of Aaron. Thus Joseph was obligated to present him to the Lord and pay the price of his redemption.

The deep irony is that Joseph and Mary pay the ransom to redeem their son, who himself is the Redeemer of the world. They redeem him from a lifetime of service as a priest of the Lord, when he has come as the great High Priest who offers the one, full, perfect, and sufficient sacrifice for the sins of the whole world.

For Joseph, the price of redeeming his son is five silver shekels. For Jesus, the price of redeeming the world will be his very life, offered up on the cross. The aged Simeon clearly recognizes this redemptive vocation in his prophetic words concerning the child and his mother: "This child is destined for the falling and the rising of many in Israel, and to be a sign that will be opposed so that the inner thoughts of many will be revealed—and a sword will pierce your own soul too."

By the payment of five silver shekels, the world's Redeemer is redeemed. This image foreshadows the greatest mystery of all. Just as the priest hands the infant Jesus back to Joseph, returning him to the life of his earthly family, so, having paid the price of our redemption on the cross, Jesus returns from the tomb as the bearer of eternal life for all who become his new family in the kingdom of God.

December 30

The Daughter of Phanuel, of the Tribe of Asher

1 John 2:12-17
Psalm 96:7-10
Luke 2:36-40

During the season of Advent, the Sunday and weekday eucharistic readings prominently featured prophecies of the coming of the messiah. In Luke's account of the Presentation of Jesus in the temple, the figures of Simeon and Anna represent this tradition of Old Testament prophecy. Encountering the infant Jesus, they recognize the fulfillment of God's promises and proclaim the arrival of the one for whom they have been waiting.

Some commentators suggest that Luke is careful to mention not just one but two prophets because of the Old Testament law that only the testimony of two or more witnesses is valid. Others suggest that the combined testimony of the man, Simeon, and the woman, Anna, achieves a degree of wholeness and completeness indicating that Jesus has come as the savior of all people.

Since Luke does not report the words of Anna, however, she is apt to be overlooked. We do well to consider what the biblical text tells us about her and also what it may imply without saying explicitly.

Well advanced in years, Anna and Simeon embody the ancient messianic hopes and dreams of the nation. Anna was a widow. The text is not totally clear about her age, but the New Revised Standard Version is likely correct in its rendering that she was eighty-four years old, having lived most of her life as a widow after a marriage of seven years.

Early Christian commentators made much of Anna's extended widowhood, since widows exercised an important quasi-official office in the church. Freed from the concerns of family life, Anna had time to fast and pray daily in the temple. The early church held her up as a positive example to Christians in general and to Christian widows in particular.

Luke identifies Anna as the daughter of Phanuel of the tribe of Asher. We know nothing else of Phanuel. The tribe of Asher was, however, one of the "ten lost tribes" of the northern kingdom of Israel, deported by the Assyrians in about 722 BCE. It is possible that even seven centuries later some inhabitants of Jerusalem could still trace their ancestry to one or another of the lost tribes. But it seems more likely to me that this designation is symbolic: Anna's genealogy embodies the Jewish hope for a re-gathering of the tribes of Israel in the messianic kingdom that Jesus has come to inaugurate. (Jesus himself later appoints twelve apostles as a symbol of this very re-gathering of the "Lost Sheep" of the house of Israel.)

The figure of Anna may also harken back, by way of allusion, to another woman of the tribe of Asher mentioned in the Old Testament: Serah. A daughter of Asher, one of the twelve sons of Jacob, Serah is recorded among the seventy members of Jacob's family who migrated from Canaan to Egypt (Genesis 46:17). A number of legends developed about her in rabbinic tradition. According to one, she was the first to tell her grandfather Jacob that Joseph was still alive in Egypt; in return, Jacob blessed her with eternal (or at least very long) life. Still alive in the time of the Exodus, she verified to the elders of Israel that Moses was the one appointed by God to deliver Israel from bondage in Egypt. And Moses learned from Serah the location of Jacob's bones so that they could be taken for burial in the promised land.

Precisely on account of her great age, Serah figures in rabbinic tradition as a personification of the people's corporate memories and hopes. Just as the daughter of Asher recognizes Moses as the liberator of Israel, so the daughter of Phanuel recognizes the infant Jesus as the savior and so acclaims him to all who are looking for the redemption of Jerusalem. This is not to say that

Luke identifies Anna with Serah directly; nonetheless, the figure of Serah looms large in the background of his telling of the story.

The encounter of Simeon and Anna with the infant Jesus—known in Eastern Orthodoxy as "the Meeting"—makes a simple point. The ancient prophecies had foretold a messiah who would be the agent of God's kingdom on earth. Personified in Simeon and Anna, this tradition of prophecy proclaims the fulfillment of this hope in Jesus, as Mary and Joseph bring him into God's temple—indeed, his own temple—for the first time.

December 31

And the Word Became Flesh

1 John 2:18-21
Psalm 96:1-2, 11-13
John 1:1-18

(Note: Today's gospel is also that for the Third Proper for Christmas Day, and the First Sunday of Christmas.)

It is a bit ironic, but not at all inappropriate, that on the last day of the secular year, the gospel reading takes us back to the beginning. The prologue to the Gospel of John has been read at the third service of Christmas and again on the First Sunday after Christmas. In some parishes of an Anglo-Catholic tradition it is still read as "the Last Gospel" following the Holy Eucharist at least during the Christmas season, but in some places year-round. We do well to return to it often and meditate on its mystery.

"In the beginning was the Word, and the Word was with God, and the Word was God." The phrase "in the beginning" harks back deliberately to the first verse of the Book of Genesis, before the beginning of creation. Even then, "the

Word" (*Logos*) existed with God and "was God." In the early centuries of Church history, Christian theology recognized this Word as the second person of the Holy Trinity, God the Son, who has existed from all eternity, together with the Father and the Holy Spirit.

To call this second person of the Trinity "the Word" reveals something crucially important about God. The Judeo-Christian God is, above all, a God who speaks. Self-communication, self-revelation, self-disclosure is intrinsic to the divine nature. God speaks first of all in creation itself: "All things came into being through [the Word]; and without [the Word] not one thing came into being."

God's Word, moreover, is life and light to all people: "The light shines in the darkness, and the darkness did not overcome it." Implicit in these lines is the idea that God's eternally pre-existent Word is expressed, first, in God's creation and, second, in God's self-revelation in the Law and the Prophets. Again and again, the prophets of Israel begin their discourses with the phrase, "The Word of the Lord came to me…"

During Advent we noted the close linkage and complementarity between the ministries of Jesus and John the Baptist. Significantly, the prologue gives a place of prominence to John as a "man sent from God…to testify to the light…"

So we see a progression. The Word is, first, in the beginning with God, then active in the creation of the universe, then revealed in the Law and the Prophets, culminating in John the Baptist. Finally, as God's supreme act of self-communication, this self-same Word comes into the created universe as a human being, initially incognito and unrecognized: "He was in the world, and the world came into being through him; yet the world did not know him."

His presence in the world does not meet with universal recognition and acceptance, even among his own people: "He came to what was his own, and his own people did not accept him." Yet some people do recognize and believe in his Name. To these he gives power "to become children of God."

The discourse reaches its climax in the ringing affirmation: "And the Word became flesh and lived among us, and we have seen his glory, the glory as of the father's only son, full of grace and truth." In many congregations, when these words are read the people genuflect as a sign of reverence for the mystery they proclaim.

The branch of theology that seeks to understand who Jesus is, the person of Christ, is called Christology. Theologians sometimes make a distinction between what they call a "high" Christology emphasizing Jesus' divinity and a "low" Christology emphasizing his humanity.

But the prologue blends high and low Christologies perfectly. Jesus is the eternally pre-existent Logos, the fully divine Son of God. Yet in the Incarnation, he becomes flesh and dwells among us, partaking fully of our created human nature.

The word "flesh," in Greek *sarx*, highlights the sheer materiality of human existence in all the organic splendor of its biological processes, bodily fluids, viscera, excreta, blood-and-guts, skin-and-bones. It was this that the Word became, and it was through this—in the cradle and from the cross—that his divine glory shone.

By thus sharing in our human nature, the Word-made-flesh becomes the source of "grace and truth" to human beings. Early Christian theologians such as Athanasius of Alexandria developed this idea to suggest that by partaking in our human nature, God the Son enables us to partake of the divine nature and thus live with God for eternity.

The prologue concludes, "No one has ever seen God. It is God the only Son, who is close to the Father's heart, who has made him known." Here we have come full circle; the designation "Word" (Logos) for the Son of God implies an inescapably self-communicative dimension of divine Being. By ourselves, we cannot see or know God. But in the beginning was the Word. Self-revelation is intrinsic to

God's nature, as is the self-communication of grace and truth to all creatures, even to the extent of sending the Son to share in their fleshly life, and to die on a cross, that they might share forever in the life of God.

The Holy Name of Our Lord Jesus Christ

January 1

Numbers 6:22-27
Psalm 8
Galatians 4:4-7 or Philippians 2:5-11
Luke 2:15-21

In editions of *The Book of Common Prayer* prior to 1979, today's feast was commemorated as the Circumcision of Christ, which took place according to the Torah, eight days after Jesus' birth. While commemorating the formal naming of Jesus on the same occasion, the Feast of the Holy Name has a somewhat different emphasis. The preacher has the opportunity today to focus on one of a number of different themes: the shedding of Christ's blood at his circumcision; the obedience of his parents to the Jewish law; the etymological significance of the name Jesus; and the power of the Holy Name for those who believe.

The Second Sunday after Christmas

Jeremiah 31:7-14
Psalm 84 or 84:1-8
Ephesians 1:3-6, 15-19a
Matthew 2:13-15, 19-23 or Luke 2:41-52 or Matthew 2:1-12

The Second Sunday after Christmas is celebrated liturgically only in those years when it falls before the Feast of the Epiphany on January 6. In these years, it always falls between January 2 and 5, and its proper readings take precedence over those appointed for the weekday of the same date.

The gospel readings on this Sunday give the preacher a wide scope of choice among alternative themes associated with the infancy narratives. The first gospel reading, from Matthew, recounts the flight of the Holy Family into Egypt following Herod's slaughter of the innocents of Bethlehem. The reading from Luke tells the story of the youthful Jesus being lost and found in the Temple. The third gospel reading, Matthew 2:1-12, presents the visit of the Magi, and effectively gives the preacher permission to anticipate the Epiphany.

January 2

Among You Stands
One Whom You Do Not Know

I John 2:22-29
Psalm 98:1-5
John 1:19-28

(Note: The first readings for the weekdays between January 2 and 12 are taken in sequence from the First Epistle of John. Some overlapping readings in I John are appointed for the Sundays of Easter in Year B. Today's gospel reading overlaps with that appointed for the Third Sunday of Advent, Year B.)

But this is where we came in! Already it is day nine of the Twelve Days of Christmas, and it suddenly seems as if we've gone back to the Second Week of Advent with more about John the Baptist! True, for the next few days the gospel readings once again feature John the Baptist. But we are in a different place from where we were in the middle of December for two reasons.

First, during Advent, the gospel readings about John were taken from the three synoptic gospels of Matthew, Mark, and Luke. Today, and in the coming days, they are from the Gospel of John, which gives a somewhat different perspective.

Second, the seasonal context is different. During Advent, we were looking at John primarily in his ministry of calling people to repentance anticipating the imminent arrival of the messiah and the kingdom of God. The emphasis was on the future. Today, we begin looking at John in anticipation of the Baptism of Christ on the First Sunday after the Epiphany. The readings focus on John's witness after Jesus has arrived at the River Jordan. The emphasis is on the present.

The fourth gospel's account of Jesus at the River Jordan is divided into four days. Beginning today, the weekday lectionary assigns the gospel readings for each of these days to January 2, 3, 4, and 5 respectively. So we begin today on day one.

The day's action is taken up with John's response to a delegation of priests and scribes sent to him from Jerusalem. Their first question is, "Who are you?" Without waiting to be asked, John immediately confesses: "I am not the Messiah." John understands that before he can give a positive account of who he is, he must first clarify who he is not. His questioners have preconceived notions of who he must be claiming to be by behaving as he does—either the messiah, or Elijah, or the prophet—and he must defuse their preconceptions before they will be able to hear his answer to their questions.

Both Elijah and the prophet were figures from Old Testament prophecy who were expected to arrive as precursors to the messiah. The expectation of Elijah's return was based on Malachi 4:5, "Lo, I will send you the prophet Elijah before the great and terrible day of the LORD comes." And Moses foretells the prophet in his parting words in Deuteronomy 18:15: "The LORD your God will raise up for you a prophet like me from among your own people…" Although in the synoptic gospels Jesus later affirms that John is the returned Elijah, the Baptist of the fourth gospel entertains no such ideas about himself. He denies in turn that he is the messiah, Elijah, or the prophet.

His questioners then logically ask: "Who are you? Let us have an answer for those who sent us. What do you say about yourself?" John's answer draws on Isaiah 40:3: he is the mysterious voice crying in the wilderness, "Make straight the way of the Lord." Rather than try to understand this answer on its own terms, however, his questioners fall back on their preconceived categories. "Why then are you baptizing if you are neither the Messiah, nor Elijah, nor the prophet?"

John's response, "I baptize with water," clarifies that whatever his baptism means, it is not the sign of messianic pretensions that his questioners think it is. What he says next can be paraphrased in the words of a suspect being interrogated in a detective novel: "Look, you've got the wrong guy! You don't even know who you're really looking for, even though he's right in front of your noses!"

John's actual words, "Among you stands one whom you do not know," contain the tantalizing hint that Jesus is already present in the crowd standing by, listening to this exchange. But for today he remains unknown, an anonymous presence on the banks of the Jordan.

The episode is illustrative of a principle in the Christian spiritual life known as the *via negativa*, or the way of negation. Before we can open ourselves up to God's truth, we must allow God to dispel our preconceived notions that contradict or fall short of that truth. Before John the Baptist can say who he is, he must first say who he is not. And even when he answers the question of who he is, he must immediately add that it's really the wrong question, for he's not the important person in this picture. Before we can begin to know Christ, we must first acknowledge that we really don't know him: that he stands among us as one unknown. Only then can we open ourselves up to receive him as he really is.

January 3

I Saw the Spirit Descending from Heaven like a Dove

1 John 3:1-6
Psalm 98:1-2, 4-7
John 1:29-34

(Note: Today's gospel overlaps with that appointed for the Second Sunday after the Epiphany, Year A.)

Alone of the four gospels, the Gospel according to John does not explicitly describe the baptism of Christ. In today's gospel reading, the baptism has already happened.

John the Baptist appears not to have known who Jesus was until the moment when he came up out of the water and the Holy Spirit descended upon him in the form of a dove. Hence John declares twice, "I myself did not know him." And then he continues: "I saw the Spirit descending from heaven like a dove, and it remained on him…the one who sent me to baptize with water said to me, 'He on whom you see the Spirit descend and remain is the one who baptizes with the Holy Spirit.'"

In this gospel reading, Jesus is revealed to John, and John in turn bears witness to Jesus. In so doing, John makes a number of different affirmations about who Jesus is and what he does.

According to John's testimony in this short passage, Jesus is, first, the Lamb of God who takes away the sin of the world. Second, he is the one who although coming after John ranks before him because he was before him (which hints at Jesus' pre-existence). Third, Jesus is the one on whom the Spirit has descended and remained. Fourth, he is the one who baptizes with the Holy Spirit and, fifth, the Son of God.

It would be possible to preach an entire sermon on any one of these titles. For today, however, we'll focus on one image in particular: the descent of the dove. "And John testified, 'I saw the Spirit descending from heaven like a dove, and it remained on him.'"

This image of the dove alludes to the opening verses of Genesis, where the Spirit hovers over the primordial waters, like a brooding bird waiting to hatch her young. There may also be an allusion to the story of Noah, where the dove returns to the ark over the waters bearing an olive leaf as a sign that the waters are subsiding and final deliverance from the deluge is near.

In the language of biblical symbolism, the waters of the Jordan evoke the waters of primordial chaos, which in the Book of Genesis pre-existed an ordered creation—and which, in the deluge at the time of Noah threatened once again to engulf and destroy the world.

At his baptism, Jesus descends into the waters of the Jordan, and the Spirit descends upon him in the likeness of the dove. Just as the Spirit hovered over the waters in the beginning, so now, the descending dove points to Jesus as the agent of a new creation. Jesus emerges from the waters just as the dry land emerged from the waters in the beginning of creation, and again after the deluge in the time of Noah.

The imagery may evoke ancient mythology that goes back further than the Book of Genesis. Many scholars believe that Mesopotamian creation myths provided the background for the creation story in the first chapter of Genesis. In some of these myths, a god or divine hero, Marduk, fights and kills a sea monster, Tiamat, and fashions the dry land out of her carcass. The underlying premise is that before an ordered creation can emerge, the evil resident in the watery chaos must be defeated. Genesis dispenses with the Mesopotamian deities in the narrative and substitutes the figure of the God of Israel subduing the primordial chaos of the waters to bring into being a cosmos that is "very good."

If this account of the background and associations of Genesis is accurate, then the descent of Christ into the waters of the Jordan assumes momentous significance. Jesus recapitulates the figure of the divine hero who defeats the evil resident in the primordial chaos so that he can bring a new creation into being.

Christ's descent into the waters points to at least two other descents. Already, he has descended from heaven to earth to defeat the forces of sin and death which hold humanity captive. Following his death on the cross, he will descend into hell to break the power of the devil and liberate those held captive by death. These three descents—from heaven to be born as a human infant at Christmas, into the waters of the Jordan at his baptism, and into the nether regions of the earth on Holy Saturday—are all parts of the same downward movement of the Son of God to gather up fallen humanity and lift us up to our true home in heaven.

January 4

Here Is the Lamb of God
1 John 3:7-10
Psalm 98:1-2:8-10
John 1:35-42

(Note: Today's gospel overlaps with that appointed for the Second Sunday after the Epiphany, Year A.)

In The Episcopal Church's sanctoral calendar—that is, the calendar of saints' days—today is the commemoration of Elizabeth Ann Seton, founder of the American Sisters of Charity and the first citizen of the United States to be canonized in the Roman Catholic Church. In the Church's temporal calendar—that is, the calendar of times and seasons—today is the Eleventh Day of Christmas.

The daily eucharistic readings in these weekdays of early January look ahead to the celebration of the Baptism of Christ, the feast concluding the Christmas-Epiphany Season. They help us explore the mystery of the Incarnation by looking at the witness borne to Jesus by John the Baptist at the River Jordan.

In today's gospel, Jesus has already been baptized, and John has recognized him as the Son of God by the Holy Spirit descending and remaining on him. The next day, speaking to two of his disciples, John describes Jesus as "the Lamb of God." John's witness sets in motion a sequence by which the two follow Jesus and listen to his teaching. One of the two, Andrew, finds his brother Simon and brings him to Jesus, who declares that henceforth he will be known as Cephas, or Peter. Already, the gathering of disciples is underway as people follow Jesus, listen to him, and bring others to him.

John's declaration that Jesus is "the Lamb of God" discloses a deep insight into who Jesus is and what he has come to do. The biblical image of the lamb was multi-layered. In the Old Testament, lambs were routinely presented for sacrifice by individual Israelites to take away the guilt of sin. Then there was the Passover lamb, whose blood on the doorposts of the Hebrews' houses in Egypt kept away the angel of death. Thirdly, the lamb was also a figure of the suffering servant in the Book of Isaiah: "He was oppressed, and he was afflicted, yet he opened not his mouth; like a lamb that is led to the slaughter, and like a sheep that before its shearers is silent, so he did not open his mouth" (Isaiah 53:7).

In this way, even as Jesus makes his first appearance in the pages of the gospels, by calling him "the Lamb of God" John points to his sacrificial death on the cross as the reason why he has come into the world. It is sometimes said that the cross overshadows even the scene of the nativity in Bethlehem.

This message might seem overly somber, except for one further consideration. In the Bible, the lamb is a symbol not only of sacrifice, but also of feasting and celebration. In the ancient world, if you wanted to have a good party, you'd roast a lamb or maybe multiple lambs. At the end of the New Testament, the Revelation to John follows through on this imagery with the joyful acclamation, "Blessed are those who are invited to the marriage supper of the Lamb" (Revelation19:9).

In some Episcopal Churches in the Anglo-Catholic tradition, at the moment of showing the consecrated host and chalice to the people, the priest proclaims the words of John the Baptist: "Behold, the Lamb of God. Behold him who takes away the sin of the world." Jesus is the sacrificial lamb who takes away our sins and gives himself to us in the Holy Eucharist as our spiritual food and drink. The Eucharist, in turn, gives us a foretaste of the messianic banquet, the marriage supper of the lamb to which we're all invited.

January 5

An Israelite in Whom There Is No Deceit
1 John 3:11-18
Psalm 100
John 1:43-51

(Note: Today's gospel overlaps with that appointed for the Second Sunday after the Epiphany, Year B.)

The gospel readings for January 2 through 5 are taken from the first chapter of John's Gospel. The setting is the River Jordan, where John the Baptist is baptizing. Jesus has come for baptism and John has borne witness to him as the Lamb of God who takes away the sin of the world. And Jesus has begun to gather his first disciples, including Andrew and Simon Peter.

These events at the Jordan are spread out over four days. Today's gospel comprises day four, and begins with the information that Jesus has decided to go to Galilee. He calls Philip—who has not been mentioned previously by name but is presumably one of the disciples who listened to his teaching the previous day—and he bids him, "Follow me."

Philip in turn calls Nathanael and says to him, "We have found him about whom Moses in the law and also the prophets wrote, Jesus son of Joseph from Nazareth." Some commentators make the observation that from the perspective of the fourth gospel, Philip's description of Jesus is partially true but incomplete. He is the one about whom Moses and the prophets wrote. But his identity cannot be limited to his lineage, "son of Joseph," or his hometown Nazareth. To try to define him in these terms is to circumscribe one's vision of who he really is.

According to this interpretation, Nathanael's response, "Can anything good come out of Nazareth?"—an expression perhaps of cosmopolitan Judean prejudices against the backwaters of Galilee—unwittingly pinpoints the inadequacy of Philip's description.

Rather than arguing, Philip wisely invites Nathanael to "Come and see." Upon seeing Nathanael coming toward him, Jesus remarks, "Here is truly an Israelite in whom there is no deceit!" It is a fitting description of Nathanael's character as revealed in his previous blunt question about anything good coming out of Nazareth. Nathanael is clearly someone who says what he thinks.

Nathanael's response, "Where did you get to know me?"—is less than respectful. He rudely omits any courteous form of address, such as "Rabbi," or "Sir." He is implicitly challenging Jesus: Who are you to think that you know me well enough to make any such assessment? Unwittingly, however, he is focusing and raising to a new level of urgency the question at the heart of today's gospel: Who is Jesus?

Scholars have debated many possible interpretations of Jesus' answer, often involving the significance of fig trees in the Hebrew scriptures. The important point, however, is that Jesus' words are sufficient to convince Nathanael that Jesus has supernatural knowledge of his private doings. Nathanael's attitude is completely reversed as he acclaims Jesus with titles reserved for the messiah: "Rabbi, you are the Son of God! You are the King of Israel!"

The story could easily end here, but it does not. The titles "Son of God" and "King of Israel" are true, but still inadequate to convey the full reality of who Jesus is. So Jesus asks Nathanael: "Do you believe because I told you that I saw you under the fig tree? You will see greater things than these…Very truly, I tell you, you will see heaven opened and the angels of God ascending and descending upon the Son of Man."

The image of heaven opened and the angels of God ascending and descending alludes to the story of Jacob's ladder in Genesis 28. On his travels, Jacob dreamed that he saw a ladder from earth to heaven, and the angels of God ascending and descending on it. When he awoke, he exclaimed, "Surely the LORD is in this place and I did not know it!…How awesome is this place! This is none other than the house of God, and this is the gate of heaven" (Genesis 28:16-17). Jacob then set up a stone to mark the spot and called the place Bethel, "House of God."

Rearranging the imagery slightly, Jesus identifies himself as the place where the angels of God ascend and descend: "Very truly, I tell you, you will see heaven opened and the angels of God ascending and descending upon the Son of Man." Jesus is the new meeting place of heaven and earth. He is the new "Gate of Heaven," the new "House of God," and perhaps the new ladder between earth and heaven as well. The "greater things" to be seen by those who follow him are precisely God's self-revelations in and through Jesus' words and deeds.

For Philip and Nathanael, Andrew and Simon Peter, an unsurpassed adventure is about to begin as they journey to Galilee. So it is for all who respond to Jesus' call to follow him.

The Epiphany

January 6

Isaiah 60:1-6
Psalm 72:1-7, 10-14
Ephesians 3:1-12
Matthew 2:1-12

In early Christian tradition, the Feast of the Epiphany focused simultaneously on three distinct events in Jesus' life: the visit of the Magi bearing their gifts of gold, frankincense, and myrrh; the baptism of Jesus in the River Jordan; and the transformation of water into wine at the wedding feast of Cana. Only gradually did the January 6 feast come to be focused on the first of these, and then only in the western Church; so that a separate Feast of the Baptism of Our Lord was instituted for the Sunday following January 6.

The weekday eucharistic lectionary is predicated on the understanding that both the Epiphany and the Baptism of Christ mark not so much the beginning of a new Epiphany season as the culmination and climax of the Christmas season or, what might be called the "Christmas-Epiphany season." The readings and homilies in the following pages for January 7 through 12 are used only on the weekdays before the Baptism of Our Lord. On the Monday following the Baptism of Our Lord, we are back in "ordinary time," and the daily lectionary for the weekdays following the Sundays after the Epiphany is used instead.

January 7

Jesus Begins His Ministry in Galilee

1 John 3:18-4:6
Psalm 2
Matthew 4:12-17, 23-25

(Note: Today's gospel overlaps with that appointed for the Third Sunday after the Epiphany, Year A.)

Yesterday we celebrated the Epiphany. From today until the celebration of the Baptism of Our Lord on Sunday, our gospel readings dwell on what might be called "minor epiphanies"—events or activities in which Jesus' identity as the Messiah and Son of God is made manifest to those who witness them.

Today's gospel reading begins, logically enough, at the beginning of Jesus' public ministry in Galilee. According to Matthew, when John the Baptist is arrested, Jesus withdraws to Galilee and makes his home at Capernaum by the Sea. He begins to travel throughout Galilee, proclaiming the good news of the kingdom of God and performing miraculous healings. These activities alone constitute an epiphany of sorts by beginning to bring Jesus to public attention.

The evangelist Matthew describes Jesus' residence in Capernaum as the fulfillment of a prophecy of Isaiah:

Land of Zebulun, land of Naphtali,
    on the road by the sea, across the Jordan,
Galilee of the Gentiles—the people who sat in darkness
    have seen a great light,
and for those who sat in the region and shadow of death
    light has dawned (Matthew 4:15-16).

Zebulun and Naphtali were two of the twelve sons of Jacob. When Joshua led the Israelites across the Jordan into the promised land, the tribes of Zebulun and Naphtali received their territories in the northernmost region, in the area that would eventually become known as Galilee.

These territories of Zebulun and Naphtali were the first to be conquered by the Assyrians in 732 BCE, nine years before the rest of the northern kingdom of Israel in 723. At the time of this catastrophe, Isaiah uttered the prophecy quoted in today's gospel. Even though a great darkness has descended upon Zebulun and Naphtali, and Galilee has become subject to the nations, nonetheless God will have the last word. Speaking as though it's already happened, the prophet announces a great reversal: "The people who sat in darkness have seen a great light, and for those who sat in the region and shadow of death, light has dawned."

Whatever Isaiah may have understood by this prophecy, it wasn't fulfilled in his lifetime. The ten tribes whose territories constituted the northern kingdom of Israel were deported and disappeared from history. The lands of Zebulun and Naphtali remained under Gentile control for centuries—first the Assyrians, then the Babylonians, then the Persians, and then the Greeks.

Only when the independent Jewish kingdom of the Maccabees gained control of the area in the first century BCE did Jews re-colonize Galilee, some 600 years after the Assyrian conquests. These Jewish settlers established the towns whose names feature so prominently in the gospels, such as Nazareth, Cana, and Capernaum. The area came under Gentile control once again in 37 BCE when the Roman general Pompey conquered Palestine. But by this time a permanent Jewish presence was established in Galilee, the territory of Zebulun and Naphtali.

So, when Jesus returns to Galilee after his baptism and begins to preach the kingdom of God, the evangelist Matthew discerns the fulfillment of the ancient prophecy of Isaiah. For Matthew, the area is "Galilee of the Gentiles" because it's a place where Jewish towns and settlements exist alongside Gentile towns and settlements. The Jews of Galilee seem to have had the reputation of not being very knowledgeable in the Law or observant in their religious practice. To their co-religionists in Judea, Galilee seemed a place of darkness. Matthew's point is that when God appears on the scene and acts in history, it is often done in the least likely and most unexpected places—not initially in the great metropolis of Jerusalem, the religious and administrative center of the nation, but up north, in a rural backwater of remote farms and fishing villages.

Jesus' public ministry in Galilee—his preaching, teaching, healings, miracles, and calling of disciples—represents the dawning of God's light on those who sit in darkness. The good news of today's gospel, then, is that no matter what form the darkness may take for us, Jesus is the one who brings us light. He is the one who illumines our lives with the radiance of divine glory and delivers us from the shadow of death.

January 8

Feeding the Five Thousand
1 John 4:7-12
Psalm 72:1-8
Mark 6:30-44

(Note: Today's gospel overlaps with that appointed for Proper 11, Year B.)

The feeding of the five thousand is one of the classic epiphanies of Jesus' divine identity as the Son of God. Recorded in all four gospels, it is clearly a miraculous event: five loaves and two fish multiply to feed five thousand people.

Reductionist explanations of "a miracle of sharing"—in which the disciples' offering what little food they have inspires all those in the crowd who have food to share it with their neighbors—belong to the rationalist mindset of the eighteenth-century Enlightenment, which rules out *a priori* any possibility of the genuinely miraculous. They certainly do not belong to the biblical mindset. And if our God is the sort of God our Church professes, these rationalizations do not belong to our mindset, either. We need not be scandalized by the miraculous.

Mark's account shows an interesting process of interaction between Jesus and the disciples in responding to the crisis engendered by the lack of food for the multitude. The disciples initially identify the problem. Large numbers of people have followed Jesus out into the wilderness to listen to his teachings. It's getting late. So the disciples approach Jesus and ask him to send the crowds away to the surrounding villages so they can buy food for themselves.

Precisely in response to this need identified by the disciples, Jesus issues the command: "You give them something to eat." A similar pattern often is true in the Christian life: We perceive a need; we take it to Jesus and tell him what we think he ought to do about it; and he responds by telling us what he wants us to do about it!

Initially, the disciples find his response an overwhelming challenge. "Are we to go and buy two hundred denarii worth of bread, and give it to them to eat?" The question is ironic, even sarcastic. A denarius is the day's wage of a laborer. There's no way that the disciples would be carrying such a large sum of money as two hundred denarii. And transporting such a huge delivery of bread to this remote place would require several oxcarts at minimum. So, the disciples' initial response is one of outright dismissal.

But Jesus is unfazed. He won't take no for an answer. He simply asks, "How many loaves have you? Go and see." This stocktaking has great significance. Jesus wants to learn—more precisely, he wants the disciples to learn—what resources they have available. Even though it's well within his power to create loaves of bread from the rocks lying on the ground, he chooses instead to make full use of what the disciples have to offer. They must offer all that they have, holding nothing back. All five loaves and two fish: nothing less will do.

What I find enormously reassuring in this story, however, is that it's precisely the gifts that the disciples actually have that Jesus takes and works with. He doesn't fault them for not having brought more food. The five loaves and two fish will do nicely. Nothing less will do, but nothing more is needed.

That's a point we need to remember whenever we're tempted to envy the gifts that others have received and that we haven't. God has given each of us a unique set of talents given to no one else. It's precisely those gifts, rather than someone else's, that God wants us to offer in service. If God has given one person the ability to paint but not sing, fine. If God has given another person a warm, empathetic personality but no head for math, fine. We're always tempted to focus on and bewail the qualities we lack. We're always tempted to think that God wants us to become someone other than who we are. But what God really wants for us is to become more fully ourselves, to offer God not the gifts that we don't have, but rather those that we do have: our own five loaves and two fish.

The outcome of the story is that when Jesus takes the five loaves and two fish, he accomplishes something that is humanly impossible. It is an epiphany of his divine power. Similarly, however insignificant or inadequate our gifts may seem in relation to the overwhelming needs around us, when we offer them in God's service, and hold nothing back, God will do greater things with them than we can ask or imagine.

January 9

Walking on Water
1 John 4:11-19
Psalm 72:1-2, 10-13
Mark 6:45-52

(Note: Today's gospel overlaps with that appointed for Proper 11, Year B.)

Most scholars believe that the Gospel according to Mark was the first of the four canonical gospels to have been written, and that Matthew and Luke used his narrative as a source while expanding and developing it. Others think that Mark wrote after Matthew and Luke, giving an edited-down and condensed summary of the story they had told in more detail. Either way, Matthew's and Luke's versions of events tend to be more elaborate, while Mark's tends to be more spare.

Jesus walking across the Sea of Galilee is a case in point. Missing from Mark's account are any such details as Peter trying and failing to walk on the water. Instead, Mark gives us the summary outline. After feeding the five thousand, Jesus bids his disciples to get into the boat and cross to the other side of the lake, while he goes up on a mountain by himself to pray. Even though it's dark and they're miles away, well out of sight, he can see that they're having a hard time, for the wind is against them. So, he comes to them, walking across the sea.

Then Mark says something quite puzzling: "He intended to pass them by." Why would Jesus mean to pass the disciples by if his purpose in walking out on the water is to aid them in their distress? Surely he's not just taking a shortcut to get to the other side ahead of them? What's going on here?

He meant to pass by them. That phrase echoes several Old Testament passages where God "passes by." In the Book of Exodus, Moses goes up on Mount Sinai to receive the Law; and he asks God, "Show me your glory, I pray." But the Lord responds, "You cannot see my face; for no one shall see me and live." But then the Lord God tells Moses to stand in a cleft in the rock; so that when he passes by Moses will see God's back but not God's face.

Again, in the Book of 1 Kings, the Prophet Elijah flees to Mount Horeb and hides in a cave. God tells him to go out and stand upon the mount. Then, the text reads, "[The word of the Lord] said, 'Go out and stand on the mountain before the Lord, for the Lord is about to pass by.' Now there was a great wind, so strong that it was splitting mountains and breaking rocks in pieces"

(1 Kings 19:11). Clearly, the Lord passing by is an awesome and dangerous event. But as its result, both Moses and Elijah are strengthened and encouraged for the challenges that lie ahead.

In light of these Old Testament uses of the term, it seems reasonable to infer that when Mark tells us that Jesus intended to "pass by" the disciples, he's not saying that Jesus intended to go on ahead to the other shore, but rather that he intended to come near, to show himself. The purpose of his walking on the water is not so much to mount a rescue-at-sea operation—though that element is not absent—as it is to manifest his divine glory as he passes near his disciples in the boat.

The disciples don't get it. Thinking that they're seeing a night specter, a phantom, a ghost—which would most likely portend their imminent drowning—they cry out in terror. Jesus declares: "Take heart, it is I; do not be afraid." One of the hallmarks of appearances of the divine to human beings in the Bible is a reaction of overwhelming fear, evoking in turn such words as, "Fear not," or "Be not afraid." By these words, then, Jesus reveals his divine identity. And the phrase "It is I" can equally well be translated, "I AM," God's name revealed to Moses at the burning bush.

What we have here, then, is a classic biblical account of a theophany, the appearance of God to human beings.

But the most astounding twist in the story is yet to come. Jesus gets into the boat, and the wind ceases. This supernatural figure who has come striding over the waves by night is not only fully divine but also fully human. Walking on the water manifests his divinity; getting into the boat manifests his humanity. In the person of Jesus, the same God who masters the wind and waves becomes one of us, another passenger in the boat.

Here is enormous reassurance and comfort. Think of times when God has drawn near. Perhaps there was a period when things weren't going as we'd planned, and suddenly we recognized the hand of God in events totally beyond our control. It's unnerving to realize that we're not in charge of our lives. It can be a terrifying thing to encounter the living God.

But Jesus gets into the boat with us. Moses was forbidden to look upon the face of God lest he die. But we're invited to gaze upon the face of Jesus. Then we realize that the one in charge of our lives is not only God Almighty, the omnipotent maker of heaven and earth, but also a human being like us. Jesus is able to sympathize with our weakness and help us in and through the human nature that he shares with us. And the good news in today's gospel is that in Christ God draws near and the glory of God is revealed. And then Jesus gets into the boat to bring us safely to the other shore.

January 10

At the Synagogue in Nazareth
1 John 4:19-5:4
Psalm 72:1-2, 14-19
Luke 4:14-22

(Note: Today's gospel overlaps with that appointed for the Third Sunday after the Epiphany, Year C.)

Since the twelfth century, Roman Catholics (and since the nineteenth century, some Catholic-minded Anglicans and Lutherans) have used the devotion known as the Holy Rosary as an aid to prayer and meditation. The traditional Dominican Rosary consists of fifteen "mysteries"—events in the life of Jesus and Mary—divided into three groups of five: the Joyful, Sorrowful, and Glorious Mysteries. In 2002, Pope John Paul II added a new set of five mysteries, which he called the "Luminous Mysteries" or the "Mysteries of Light."

The Joyful Mysteries correspond loosely to Advent and Christmas; the Sorrowful Mysteries to Lent and Holy Week; and the Glorious Mysteries to Eastertide. The season to which the Luminous Mysteries correspond most closely is Epiphany, because they focus on such events as Christ's Baptism, the wedding feast at Cana, and the Transfiguration—the classic gospel epiphanies manifesting Jesus' identity as the Son of God.

The third luminous mystery is perhaps the most unexpected: the Proclamation of the Kingdom of God. Today's gospel of Jesus in the synagogue at Nazareth constitutes a key moment in that proclamation.

The form of proclamation consists of the classic Jewish procedure of first reading aloud and then publicly commenting on a text from scripture. Welcomed into the synagogue in his hometown, Jesus is invited to read from the scriptures—a courtesy often extended to distinguished visitors. He is given the book of the prophet Isaiah; he finds the beautiful passage where the prophet describes his vocation as one anointed by the Holy Spirit to bring good news to the poor, release to the captives, recovery of sight to the blind, liberty to those who are oppressed—all in the acceptable year of the Lord.

But then Jesus does something unexpected and shocking. Having stood up to read, he closes the book, gives it back to the attendant, and sits down—assuming the posture of a teacher—and delivers the pronouncement: "Today this scripture has been fulfilled in your hearing."

In other words, Jesus is saying, Isaiah was not really speaking about himself but about someone who would come after him. Only now is the prophecy being fulfilled, because Jesus is the one who truly brings good news to the poor, release to the captives, sight to the blind, and liberty to those who are oppressed. The acceptable year of the Lord is now.

In this epiphany, Jesus confirms that he's the one in whom the prophecies find fulfillment. He not only proclaims the kingdom of God but also identifies himself as its bearer.

Luke describes the townspeople's reaction: "All spoke well of him." But there's also a hint of the conflict to come. They "were amazed at the gracious words that came from his mouth," and asked, "Is not this Joseph's son?" In other words, they did not quite know how to react. And in what follows, not only in Luke's account but also in Matthew's and Mark's, the townspeople take offense at him, and he makes his famous comment that no prophet is without honor except in his own country. In Luke's account, the townspeople are filled with wrath and even attempt to throw him off the brow of the hill on which their city is built.

This turn of events highlights the point that the manifestation of the Son of God in the world engenders conflict as some accept and others reject him. Jesus' own ministry shows forth the kingdom of God and yet leads to the cross. Today we commemorate William Laud, the Archbishop of Canterbury who was beheaded in 1646 after a lifetime of faithful service to Christ and his Church.

The coming of the Son of God into the world confronts each person with a choice: Shall we accept or reject him? Shall we follow him or go our own way? If we follow him, we need to be prepared to face rejection, persecution, and suffering, because his way is the Way of the Cross. Yet, paradoxically, as we discover at Easter, the cross is the ultimate manifestation of God's love and Christ's glory.

January 11

Cleansing a Leper

1 John 5:5-12
Psalm 147:13-21
Luke 5:12-16

Like Jesus' other healings, the cleansing of the leper in Luke 5 is an epiphany insofar as it helps spread the word about Jesus far and wide. Here is clearly someone with God's power to heal. Even though Jesus charges the leper to tell no one, Luke tells us, "now more than ever the word about Jesus spread abroad; many crowds would gather to hear him and be cured of their diseases."

The narrative is fairly straightforward. In one of the cities, a leper approaches Jesus and begs to be healed. Jesus grants the leper's request and cleanses him of his leprosy. Reading a little deeper, however, the story has some radical and slightly subversive undertones.

Today, the word leprosy refers exclusively to the medical condition known as Hansen's disease. By contrast, the biblical writers use the term to refer to a whole range of skin complaints, including even eczema and psoriasis. Nevertheless, in ancient Israel leprosy was one of the most dreaded diseases of all because a leper was considered ritually unclean. Notice that in the story the leper doesn't say, "If you choose, you can heal me," but rather "If you choose, you can make me clean." In other words, the leper is suffering not only from the disease itself but also from the ritual uncleanness that the disease brings upon him.

If one had leprosy, it was considered evidence that one had incurred divine displeasure. The leper was to be exiled from the community, as much for fear of unholiness and ritual pollution as for fear of physical contagion. To be a leper was to be a social outcast. Chapter 13 of the Book of Leviticus requires lepers to dwell alone in habitations outside the cities, towns, and villages, and to keep well away from anyone who doesn't have the disease.

Here we have what is known today as a boundary violation. By approaching Jesus and bowing down to the ground before him, the leper violates the distance the Law requires him to maintain. Jesus would be entirely within his rights to rebuke the leper and to get away from him as quickly as he can.

But here comes the second boundary violation. Instead of retreating, Jesus reaches out his hand and touches the leper. Now, that is unheard of, for to have any physical contact with a leper is to become ritually defiled and unclean oneself.

So we have a double boundary violation. The leper violates social, cultural, and religious restrictions by approaching Jesus, and Jesus in turn violates those same restrictions by reaching out and touching the leper. In the cultural context, such behavior is unthinkable, shocking, and scandalous.

The result, however, is the exact reverse of what would be expected. Instead of the leper making Jesus unclean, Jesus makes the leper clean. The text describes an instantaneous cure: "Immediately, the leprosy left him."

Jesus instructs the now-healed leper: "Go...and show yourself to the priest, and, as Moses commanded, make an offering for your cleansing, for a testimony to them." The standard interpretation is that by offering the required sacrifice, the former leper is giving public testimony of his cleansing so that he can be reintegrated into the life of the community.

That is true, so far as it goes. But the Greek word for "testimony," *marturion*, has a somewhat confrontational overtone. It can also be translated "witness," or "proof," and is the source of the English word "martyr." So, it's just possible that Jesus directs the leper to show himself to the priest and offer the appointed sacrifices precisely as a testimony to God's preferential love for lepers and all other such social outcasts. In this way, Jesus is announcing to the religious establishment of his day that his ministry among the tax collectors, prostitutes, sinners, and indeed lepers signals the inauguration within human history of a kingdom where healing, reconciliation, and love replace division, exclusion, and enmity.

The good news in today's gospel, then, is not only that Jesus has the power to heal us of whatever might be the equivalent of leprosy in our lives but also that he breaks down the distinctions by which we alienate ourselves from one another and oppress those who are different from us. In this way, he makes possible the realization of true community and fellowship. That prospect is radical and subversive indeed.

January 12

Final Testimony of John the Baptist
1 John 5:13-21
Psalm 149:1-4
John 3:22-30

This is a rare occasion. We use today's readings only when January 12 occurs on a Saturday that falls on the eve of the Baptism of Our Lord (that is, tomorrow). When January 12 falls after the Baptism of Our Lord, then we're back in Ordinary Time and using the calendar for the appropriate week of the year instead.

January 12 falls on the Eve of the Baptism of Our Lord only in years when the Epiphany has fallen on the previous Sunday. During the entire twenty-first century, this occurs only eleven times. That means that today's readings will be used, on average, one year in nine!

In any case, it's highly appropriate that on this last weekday of the Christmas-Epiphany season the gospel reading is the one known as the "final testimony" of John the Baptist. John figures prominently in the readings at this time of year, beginning in the Second Week of Advent and concluding with the Baptism of Our Lord tomorrow. Today we have his parting words concerning Jesus: "He must increase, but I must decrease."

In this section of John's Gospel, Jesus has just been in Jerusalem. The reading begins with Jesus and his disciples going into Judea. And here we have the one tantalizing reference in all four canonical gospels to Jesus himself baptizing. In his commentary on John's Gospel, New Testament scholar Raymond Brown suggests that Jesus' brief ministry of baptizing took place shortly after his own baptism, but that when John was arrested, Jesus withdrew to Galilee, stopped baptizing, and began a ministry focused instead on teaching and healing.

Following a discussion between John's disciples and an unnamed Jew over "purifying"—which in this context almost certainly means water purification rituals—John's disciples approach their master and complain that Jesus is now baptizing as well, "and all are going to him." They perhaps expect John to denounce Jesus for usurping his ministry, or to discuss strategies for competing with this upstart.

But John does no such thing. If all are now going to Jesus, that is the will of heaven. John never claimed to be the messiah, only the one sent before him. John's attitude is not of resignation but of joy. John likens Jesus to the bridegroom who has the bride, while he, John, is the bridegroom's friend who, standing and hearing, rejoices at the bridegroom's voice: "therefore this joy of mine is now full."

The image of the bridegroom's friend—roughly equivalent to the best man of today—draws on Jewish marriage customs of the time, which we can reconstruct to some extent from rabbinical sources. The bridegroom's friend fulfilled one (or both) of two functions.

First, prior to the wedding, the bridegroom's friend would attend to the bride, helping her to get ready for the bridegroom's arrival at her father's house (where she had continued to live since the betrothal ceremony as much as a year before). The bridegroom's friend might be the one to stand guard and announce the approach of the bridegroom who, upon arrival, would lead the bride and the entire wedding party back to his house for the marriage ceremony. In this light, John the Baptist has functioned as the bridegroom's friend by exercising a ministry of preparation, helping Israel to get ready for her bridegroom, the messiah.

Second, once the marriage ceremony had taken place under the canopy (*huppah*), the bride and groom would retire to the bridal chamber to consummate the marriage, while all the guests would wait in the precincts of the bridegroom's house. The bridegroom's friend would stand at the door of the bridal chamber. Once the marriage was consummated, the bridegroom would speak through the door to his friend, who would in turn announce the good news to all the guests standing by so that the celebrations (lasting seven days) could begin. John the Baptist may be alluding to this practice when he refers to himself as "the friend of the bridegroom, who stands and hears him [and] rejoices greatly at the bridegroom's voice."

In any case, John has now fulfilled his double ministry of preparation for, and announcement of, the bridegroom's arrival. Once the bridegroom has been united with the bride, the bridegroom's friend has nothing more to do except to rejoice along with everyone else: "He must increase, but I must decrease."

The same nuptial imagery recurs throughout the New Testament. Jesus, the Messiah, is the bridegroom; Israel—and later, the Church—is his bride. In the weeks of Ordinary Time that lie ahead, we have the opportunity to contemplate the presence of the bridegroom with the bride, as Jesus comes among his people to embody God's love for them in his teaching, preaching, and many miracles.

Further Reading

Days of the Lord: The Liturgical Year. Volume 1: Advent, Christmas, Epiphany. Collegeville: The Liturgical Press, 1991.

Nichols, Aidan, O.P. *Year of the Lord's Favour: A Homiliary for the Roman Liturgy. Volume 2: The Temporal Cycle: Advent and Christmastide, Lent and Eastertide.* Leominster, UK: Gracewing, 2012.

Nocent, Adrian. O.S.B. *The Liturgical Year. Volume 1: Advent, Christmas, Epiphany.* Collegeville: The Liturgical Press, 1977.

About the Author

John D. Alexander has been rector of St. Stephen's Episcopal Church in Providence, Rhode Island, since 2000. He previously served parishes in Wayne, Pennsylvania, and Staten Island, New York. He received his doctorate in Christian ethics from Boston University in 2014 and also holds advanced degrees from the Johns Hopkins University, Virginia Theological Seminary, and Nashotah House. He currently serves as superior of the American Region of the Society of Mary, an international devotional society in the Anglo-Catholic tradition.